KENRICK · SEMINARY · LIBRARY

CONCILIUM
Religion in the Seventies

CONCILIUM

Religion in the Seventies

EDITORIAL DIRECTORS: Edward Schillebeeckx (Dogma) · Herman Schmidt (Liturgy) · Alois Müller (Pastoral) · Hans Küng (Ecumenism) · Franz Böckle (Moral Theology) · Johannes B. Metz (Church and World) · Roger Aubert (Church History) · Teodoro Jiménez Urresti (Canon Law) · Christian Duquoc (Spirituality) · Roland Murphy (Scripture)

CONSULTING EDITORS: Marie-Dominique Chenu · ✠Carlo Colombo · Yves Congar · Andrew Greeley · Jorge Mejía · Karl Rahner · Roberto Tucci

EXECUTIVE SECRETARY: (Awaiting new appointment), Arksteestraat 3–5, Nijmegen, The Netherlands

Volume 70: Scripture

EDITORIAL BOARD: Roland Murphy · Bas van Iersel · Luis Alonso Schökel · Josef Blank · Myles Bourke · Jules Cambier · Henri Cazelles · Settimio Cipriani · Aelred Cody · José Croatto · Jacques Dupont · Joseph Fitzmeyer · José-Marie González-Ruiz · Pierre Grelot · Lucas Grollenberg · Herbert Haag · Stanislas Lyonnet · George MacRae · Martin McNamara · Salvador Muñoz Iglesias · Franz Mussner · Angelo Penna · Kazimierz Romaniuk · Heinrich Schlier · Rudolf Schnackenburg · Heinz Schürmann · David Stanley · Francis Bruce Vawter · Anton Vögtle · Thomas Worden · Silverio Zedda

THEOLOGY, EXEGESIS, AND PROCLAMATION

Volume 70

Edited by

Roland Murphy

KENRICK · SEMINARY · LIBRARY

WITHDRAWN

R
230.265
C744
v.70

Herder and Herder

721549

1971
HERDER AND HERDER NEW YORK
232 Madison Avenue, New York 10016

Cum approbatione Ecclesiastica

Library of Congress Catalog Card Number: 74–168652
Copyright © 1971 by Herder and Herder, Inc. and Stichting Concilium.
All rights reserved. Nothing contained in this publication shall be reproduced
and/or made public by means of print, photographic print, microfilm, or in
any other manner without the previous consent of the Stichting Concilium
and the publishers.

Printed in the United States

CONTENTS

PART II
BULLETIN

Editorial

THERE seems to be no end to the discussion about the place of the Bible in the whole of theology. It was, of course, particularly lively during the centuries when a division and even an antithesis existed between exegesis and theology. But the modern historical and critical methods of biblical study have revived this debate and given it a new impetus. As this number of *Concilium* is dedicated to this discussion, a few preliminary remarks are necessary.

Firstly, the word "theologian" is used not simply in the sense of the scholar who is concerned with theological research, but in the wider sense of the individual active in the life of the Church and of society, but nourished by theology. The proclamation of the biblical message therefore plays a part here. Secondly, an attempt is made to discuss the questions raised as concretely as possible. For this reason, we have included not only theoretical articles on the relationship between the Bible, exegesis and theology, but something like conversations between theologians and exegetes.

The first article is concerned with the question of the various aspects of the biblical scholar's work. Is he a theologian as well as an exegete? What is his function within the Church? Roderick MacKenzie tries to answer these and similar questions against the background of the Bible as the canon and the word of God. In another article, Gerhard Voss discusses what is involved in the relationship between exegesis and dogmatic theology. Luis

Alonso Schökel asks, in a further article, whether scienitfic exegesis is really necessary to the reader of the Bible.

One set of contributions forms, so to speak, a dialogue between a theologian and an exegete, in that the editors have invited two such specialists to make a combined contribution in each case. In the first, Gotthold Hasenhüttl and Meinrad Limbeck discuss several of the more general questions that are raised between theologians and exegetes. In his article, Bas van Iersel examines what the dogmatic theologian can do with a particular biblical text (Mark 1. 1–15), and Piet Schoonenberg provides a possible answer. In the third case, the point of departure is not one concrete text, but a biblical theme—original sin. Joseph Zalotay discusses it in the light of Scripture, and Carl Peter in the light of theology.

Between these three dialogues there are two contributions which attempt to widen the whole perspective. Bruno Dreher writes about exegesis and proclamation, and Oswald Loretz examines the situation with regard to the responsibility that the exegete has as a member of the Church and the function of the Church's magisterium in regard to the interpretation of Scripture.

In the first bulletin, Robert Ware discusses the way in which a number of contemporary theologians use the data of Scripture and the results of exegesis in their work. In the second, Jacques Audinet writes about the place of the Bible in adult catechetics.

Perhaps the best way of concluding this editorial is to quote Jacques Audinet's image—"the table is set". We very much hope that readers will benefit from the way in which the question of the relationship between the Bible, exegesis and theology is dealt with here, and from thinking about the solutions offered.

ROLAND MURPHY
BAS VAN IERSEL

PART I
ARTICLES

Roderick MacKenzie

The Self-understanding of the Exegete

AS WITH most other human activities, in exegesis practice precedes
theory. For most of us, it is easier to do it than to explain what
we are doing. And if explanations must be given, probably no
two will coincide exactly. What follows, obviously, is only one
man's attempt to give a theoretical rationale of his work. It will
stress chiefly the objective aspects of it, i.e., the conditions imposed and the methods required by the nature of the material
and the communal character of the enterprise, rather than any
subjective aspects depending on personal talents or interests of
the worker.

Up to a point, as is clear, biblical exegesis is no different from
the commentary or exposition of any ancient text, say the Code
of Hammurabi or the works of Plato. Though the commentary
as such supposes a fixed text as its subject-matter, quite frequently
there are textual uncertainties of some significance for interpretation; hence the exegete must have some skill in textual criticism, to establish the reliability of the text he is expounding.
Such linguistic competence comes next as will enable him to
understand the author's syntax and vocabulary. Then literary insight and perception of structure and patterns are required. Further, he needs historical awareness, to be able to interpret the
document in the light both of preceding and of contemporary
social or literary usages and situations. Finally, he aims at giving
an appreciation of the thought, the vision and the message, em-
bodied in his work by the ancient author; its impact on the

writer's contemporaries; and its possible relevance for our present generation.

These are the main components of the art of exegesis, as applied to ancient texts, and all have their application and importance when the text concerned is part of the Christian Bible. In practice, the word *exegesis*—as distinct, say, from the words *commentary* and *exposition*—has come to mean specifically exegesis of the Bible text. I shall use the word here in this narrow sense, and discuss the specific differences which distinguish the work of the biblical exegete who is also a believer.

There seem to be two important differences, which will affect the methods and conclusions of such an exegete. The first is the existence of the canon. The material he works on has been determined for him, by a process and an action quite different from the proceedings of the exegete himself. The canon has been fixed according to criteria extrinsic to the text; from the historical point of view it is an artificial unity, a selection from a larger body of Jewish and early Christian literature. It might have omitted some books or included others—as for example *Codex Sinaiticus* in the Old Testament omits 2 Maccabees but includes 4 Maccabees, and adds to the New Testament the Epistle of Barnabas and the Pastor of Hermas. The exegete as such has no criterion for judging canonicity; he accepts the canon or disregards it, according as he accepts or disregards the authority that fixed it. Canonicity can neither be established nor impeached on critical or exegetical grounds.

Granted then that the Christian exegete accepts the validity of the canon, how will this affect the practice of his art? How —if at all—will his handling of a canonical work differ from the treatment of non-canonical material? The theoretical answer, I believe, is this: by reason of canonicity, he will attribute to the book an extra dimension, a plus-value, over and above the values it possesses in common with other works of the same character and from the same period. His work of exegesis must be extended and continued, to include the discovery and exposition of this plus-value. More concretely: because he believes the work to contain not only words of men but also the word of God, he will endeavour to "hear" this word in the text, to understand it and to interpret it to others. If he stops short of that, his exegesis remains inadequate and incomplete. For brevity's sake, I shall refer to this last stage of the exegete's task as "theological exegesis", since it is explicitly based on faith in the Church's affirmation of the divine authority of Scripture.

This plus-value, as here described, does not take anything away from the other values—and problems—inherent in the book as words of men. All the preceding stages of criticism remain applicable to the text, and their findings duly arrived at will be valid. No modern scripturist, I believe, would question this statement, though in the past it has often enough been questioned and even denied. By an error similar to the Docetist heresy regarding the Incarnation, fervent Christians have often objected strenuously to "treating the Bible merely as a human production". But the word "merely" begs the question. The Bible is so treated only when the final stage of the exegetic process described above is neglected or refused. The earlier stages legitimately, and indeed necessarily, deal with its human aspects.

That is the theoretical answer. In practice, the matter is not quite so simple, and the separation of stages does not always work out so smoothly. The Church, through its magisterium, is competent to decide questions of doctrine, of revelation, of interpretation, belonging to the last stage mentioned above. Problems of textual criticism, as such and, for that matter, of literary and historical criticism—do not belong to divine revelation but to human research. Yet a certain overlap inevitably occurs. Church authorities may consider that a particular solution to a critical question is so bound up with some point of doctrine that to deny the former is to call in question the latter. They may accordingly issue a disciplinary instruction defending a traditional position against one newly proposed on critical grounds. They may even consider that a text-critical question has dogmatic consequences; this seems to have been the thinking which inspired the Holy Office's defence of the authenticity of the Johannine Comma in 1897.

There are graver critical questions, naturally, many of which made up the "Biblical Question" of, roughly, the first half of this century: In what sense is Moses the author of the Pentateuch? Must we conclude the multiple authorship of the book of Isaiah (and others)? When was the book of Daniel written?

Are some of the New Testament epistles pseudonymous? There is no need to discuss them here, other than to say that they are not such as can be settled by appeal to divine revelation; they belong properly to the field of literary and historical criticism. But because they have important consequences for exegesis of the respective books, the new solutions to them proposed by nineteenth-century critics had a traumatic effect on traditional schools of theology. A vast upheaval and revision of many theological conclusions were required before the Church as a whole could, so to speak, digest the new findings and their implications.

That Copernican revolution is now accomplished, and both exegetes and the magisterium are at ease with the techniques of criticism as described above. These have not, as was feared by many, proved destructive of Christian belief. On the contrary, they have enlarged and deepened in many ways the Church's understanding of the plus-value referred to, the message of God to men.

But the exegete's acceptance of the canon has a further effect at this stage of theological exegesis. By defining a collection of books and excluding all others, the Church confers on them a unity: they become the Bible. As scientific exegesis interprets one part of a book in the light of another part, and in the context of the whole, so theological exegesis interprets each book in the context of the others. This is not necessarily justifiable on critical grounds—for instance, when a later book influences the theological interpretation of an earlier one—but it is justified on theological grounds, i.e., when the complete canon is considered as the word of God.

More specifically, for the Christian exegete there is the centrality of Christ; the Old Testament, theologically, is judged in the light of the New, and in the New Testament itself the controlling norm is the person and teaching of Jesus Christ. Therefore, in theological exegesis, it is legitimate and proper to seek out and identify prophecies of Christ and of his work, in books written before his time. This principle—which is the main reason why the early Church canonized the Jewish scriptures—remains as valid now as then, for anyone who accepts the doctrine of inspiration and the consequent plus-value of inspired books. With our modern realization of historical evolution, we are naturally more conscious than were the New Testament writers, of the limited and partial nature of these prophecies. We are much more cautious in attributing the Old Testament writers any understanding of the future Salvation-bringer, beyond what can be strictly inferred from their words. But in fact they did look forward to, and affirm with certainty, a future divine intervention for the salvation of men. In all the numerous variant formulas in which that hope found expression, the Christian exegete is entitled to see some reference, however vague and unspecified, to the coming of Christ.

This brings us to the second major difference cited above, between the interpretation of canonical and that of non-canonical works. This difference is due to the binding force or moral imperative, which the exegete, like any other believer, attributes to the word of God, and which—precisely as an exegete—it is his business to interpret to his contemporary readers. This is in fact his major responsibility.

The student and interpreter of the works of other men is a critic: in a sense he judges them, even though he also learns from them. If one studies the dialogues of Plato or the *Summae* of Aquinas, one naturally expects to acquire understanding from the insights of these great minds, but one does not therefore abandon the independence of one's critical judgment. One remains free to point out limitations and defects, to doubt and even to deny. But in approaching inspired books, possessing divinely guaranteed authority, one must listen for an authoritative voice, which is not to be judged by the critic, but which judges him. When all allowances have been made for the normal human limitations of hagiographers and evangelists, there remains the towering fact that through them God is speaking. To him, men —including critics and exegetes—must listen in total humility and submission.

Men's words are conditioned and limited by their culture, period, language, etc. But God's word is free and everlasting, unconditioned and absolute. Uttered in the language of men, it is addressed to men, and it peremptorily requires a response. It may communicate *credenda*, truths to be acknowledged and affirmed, or *facienda*, choices to be made by man's free will. In either case, when God speaks, man must listen and obey. This obligation is timeless; perhaps better, it is perpetual, of all times. God's word is as binding on us as on Moses' contemporaries. Hence the existential thrust, the here-and-now validity, of the theological interpretation which the exegete must provide, when he penetrates below the time-conditioned words of men to the timeless and unconditioned word of God. Unlike his colleagues, the Platonists and Thomists, he is conveying a message which is intrinsically imperative for each of his readers.

To avoid misunderstandings, it is well to add that the distinction, words of men/word of God, is not a quantitative one. That is, we cannot mechanically separate, in the sacred text, what is stated by the narrator, or put in the mouths of men, from what is quoted as divine speech. The word of God is to be found in the crudest narratives of the book of Judges, just as it is present —no less, but also no more—in the divine speeches quoted in the Pentateuch or by the prophets. In both cases, it must be extracted from the human and time-conditioned material in which it is presented. This is the task of theological exegesis.

At this point, naturally, the exegete's own faith comes into play. It is one thing to interpret for modern men, with all possible insight and objectivity, the philosophy of a great mind or the vision of an ancient poet. Each reader remains free to judge it in his turn, to give or qualify or withhold his consent. But it is quite another thing to claim to be presenting, however feebly and imperfectly, a message which demands man's unconditioned assent. The reader who is a believer, and desirous of hearing the message, nevertheless wants an assurance of the interpreter's competence, both professional and official. The exegete who ventures on this terrain—and he must so venture, if he intends to treat the text as more than "a merely human document"—needs to establish his credentials and to declare at least implicitly the criteria by which he determines his theological interpretation.

These criteria, like canonicity, come to him from outside, and are not fixed by critical or historical science. They are fixed by the tradition of the Church. As the New Testament books themselves were produced by writers who were members of the Church and in a sense representatives of the community: as approval and canonization of their works, and of the Old Testament as well, was a sanction passed by the collective judgment

of the Church; so Christian exegesis, when it presents the contemporary religious meaning of its texts, must accord with the
faith of the Church. Ideally, it aims to express the mind of the
Church. This is the meaning of the Council of Trent's phrase
(Dz 1507): "No one should interpret ... contrary to the interpretation held by the Church". That principle is specified as re-
ferring to "matters of faith and morals", i.e., the *credenda* and
facienda, the authoritative message which is to be expounded by
the Christian exegete.

The latter, therefore, when proposing his theological exegesis,
becomes a public figure; in St Paul's terms, he has a charism to
be exercised for the building up of the Church (1 Cor. 14. 26).
He has a contribution to make, which is specifically his own, and
cannot be adequately supplied by others. He and his fellows are
the organ or faculty by which the Church meditates on, and
draws conclusion from, the written deposit of faith. His discoveries, interpretations, conclusions, are insights destined to en-
rich the Church's understanding of revelation. If exegetes were
to disappear or be no longer listened to, the ongoing life of the
Church would be gravely impoverished—which is approximately
what happened thirty years after the Modernist crisis during
the pontificate of Pius X.

On the other hand St Paul also indicates (1 Cor. 14. 29) that
the Church must critically judge the effusions of its charis-
matics, just as the Apostle is judging them and laying down rules
for their behaviour. Therefore another organ of the Church, the
magisterium, has the right and the duty, not only to receive and
listen to what the exegetes have to offer but also to regulate their
function, and to judge, finally, whether their contributions are
consonant with the doctrines hitherto held by the Church as
revealed.

Finally, we may consider the relationship between exegetes
and their fellow-workers in the service of the Church, specifically
the dogmatic theologians. Historically, as is well known, this
division is a relatively modern one; in patristic and even in
medieval times, every theologian began as an exegete, and most
of them continued thus. Modern specialization and the accumulation of sheerly factual knowledge to be mastered have necessi-
tated a certain division of labour; but it is much to be desired

that this division should not lead to separation, still less to opposition. The exegete's service to the dogmatic theologian—as to the magisterium—consists in presenting, in modern language and thought patterns, the understanding of the text that he has arrived at. This will include at least some part of the critical interpretation, on the human level; but in addition—especially when he composes a large-scale work such as a commentary or a monograph on some important theme—he will aim at giving the theological interpretation seen in the context of revelation as a whole.

To give some concrete examples: the Old Testament exegete completing a commentary on the book of Deuteronomy will indicate what he considers to be the permanently valid teaching of that book, with existential application to our own day: e.g., God's effective love for his undeserving, even rebellious creatures, the obligation of a return of love shown in action, the requirement of absolute fidelity excluding all idolatry, the constitution of a people of God which is in its way a model for the Church, and so on. The New Testament exegete expounding the Epistle to the Hebrews will similarly develop the latter's doctrine on the Incarnation, on the unique mediatorship and priesthood of Christ, on the need of perfect faith and perseverance.

It will be clear by now that the Christian exegete's work, beginning with the fundamental forms of scientific criticism, goes on to include as its final stage the work of biblical theology. That is, it aims at analysis and synthesis of some part, at least, of the authoritative divine message contained in the sacred books, and still actual for the men of our day. In so doing, he serves, among others, his colleague the dogmatic theologian, by presenting him with part of the materials to be built into his larger synthesis.

A last conclusion may be drawn from the doctrine on charisms. Each charism completes the others, and may even have to correct another. In the field of their competence, exegetes constitute the organ by which the Church does things that it cannot do, or cannot do so well, through its other members. These things may all be reduced, ultimately, to understanding of the written record of the word of God. In the words of Vatican II, "it is the task of exegetes to work according to these rules... so that through preparatory study the judgment of the Church may come to maturity" (*Dei Verbum*, 12). Exegetes have an indispensable contribution to make to the formation of that judgment, and have a right to be heard regarding its maturity or otherwise.

Gerhard Voss

The Relationship between Exegesis and Dogmatic Theology[1]

IF I had to prove that theology is a science, I could point to one characteristic at least that it has in common with other sciences. The individual theological disciplines have become almost too many to count, and there is now so much specialization that the theologian's vision is inevitably restricted to his own special field of study. There is no longer and there can no longer be such a man as the universal theologian who is equally at home in all the departments of theology. There is consequently a danger of isolation, which may not be very important as far as the historical branches of theology are concerned, and which may perhaps only result in reducing the quality of practical theology, but which throws doubt on the whole of *dogmatic theology* when this is separated from *exegesis*. This is obvious, since Scripture provides the norm for the Church's doctrines and all exegesis is in constant need of a point of orientation which must be relevant to Scripture. This orientation is provided in the first place by systematic theology, and can be regarded as more or less binding in giving direction to the exegete's interpretation of the Bible. It is clear, then, that exegetes and dogmatic theologians must together seek out the paths they are to follow. The long period during which there has been no mutual dialogue has not benefited theology.

[1] This article was originally published in *Una Sancta*, 20 (1965), pp. 101–107.

II. The Place of Exegesis

Karl Rahner has said of *Catholic* exegetes that they often seem to go about their work in the manner of secular historians or modern literary critics, "furthering knowledge of the life of Christ".[2] If dogmatic theologians are confronted with difficulties, the exegetes simply insist that these do not concern them, but only the theologians. If Rahner means by this that exegetes have to examine the *historical* facts reported in Scripture, then are they at the same time practising theology in the sense of being concerned with the words of God? Does this not presuppose that the essential matter to which Scripture bears witness is not fully expressed in Scripture itself, but that this has to be looked for, using historical and critical methods, *behind* Scripture, which in fact conceals it?

In contrast, *Protestant* exegetes have for the past forty years been opposed to this purely historical Catholic approach. Hermann Diem has said, for example: "We can and should make use of every available historical, critical and other means to become acquainted with the historical aspects of the biblical texts. *After this*, the task of *theological* exegesis begins."[3] Karl Barth wrote in the foreword to the second edition of his *Epistle to the Romans* in 1921:[4] "How what is *there* in the text is to be *understood* cannot be determined by the exegete's scattered *evaluation* of the words and word groups in the text, which is dependent on whatever point of view he happens to take. It can only be the result of the most flexible and most willing response *possible* to the inner tension present in the concepts provided with greater or lesser clarity by the text. . . . As little as possible should remain of those blocks of purely historical, purely given, purely chance concepts, and the relationship between the words and the Word must be revealed as far as possible in the words themselves."

Bultmann was also in agreement at least with Barth's intention. He believed that theologoumena cannot be separated, in the

---

[2] K. Rahner, "Exegese und Dogmatik", in H. Vorgrimler, *Exegese und Dogmatik* (Mainz, 1952), pp. 25–52, especially p. 33.

[3] H. Diem, *Dogmatik. Ihr Weg zwischen Historismus und Existentialismus* (Munich, 1955), p. 261.

[4] Munich, [4]1924, p. xii.

testimony of Scripture, from history, or that mythology cannot
be divorced from reality, so as to eliminate them. On the contrary, he thought that the intention underlying the New Testament has to be interpreted on the basis of its historically conditioned presentation of ideas. As a result, the meaning of the
phrase "historical and critical" was not the same for Bultmann
as for the nineteenth-century theologians whom Barth was chal-
lenging, and of whose work Bultmann said that, "the kerygma
itself was eliminated with the elimination of mythology".[5] Bultmann did not regard it as the aim of criticism to reconstruct a
life of Jesus behind the testimony of Scripture, but rather to
make the *testimony* of Jesus intelligible to man in the contemporary world. It is not so much his aim as the way that he carried
it out that is open to dispute.

II. The Place of Dogmatic Theology

If, then, exegesis is to occupy a central position in theology,
has dogmatic theology still any independent task to perform?
This task cannot be based, for example, on the claim that the
metaphysical concepts of dogmatic theology are more universally
valid than the biblical "statement". After all, we are not concerned in Scripture with static statements, but with historical
accounts which are "answers to concrete questions, the refutation
of concrete errors and the encouragement and admonition of concrete human beings".[6] In the same way, dogmatic statements
have also been conditioned by the prevailing view of the world,
and by a way of thinking that was current at the time of their
definition. Moreover, they often implicitly presuppose certain
premisses and conclusions. The simple fact that there are dogmas
shows that they point essentially to certain limited aspects of the
one truth revealed in Jesus Christ. We have therefore to question
the real intention of the dogmatic "statement" again and again,
as we question the biblical "statement".

[5] R. Bultmann, "Neues Testament und Mythologie", in H. W. Bartsch,
Kerygma und Mythos, I ([3]1954), pp. 15-48.
[6] E. Käsemann, "Begründet der neutestamentliche Kanon die Einheit
der Kirche?", in *Exegetische Versuche und Besinnungen*, I (Göttingen,
1960), pp. 214-23, esp. p. 217.

What, then, is the independent task that dogmatic theology has to fulfil? I believe that the theologian has to reflect upon and question the essential matter revealed by Scripture. He has, of course, to do this within the sphere disclosed by Scripture and "in constant contact with the knowledge and experience gained from this and preserved in the Church's tradition".[7] He will also attempt, in the light of this essential matter, to form a total vision of the individual statements in which the saving event of Christianity is expressed. Finally, he has the task of continuing the Church's tradition throughout history by expressing the revealed mystery of Christianity in repeated confrontations with his fellow men, and of preventing misunderstandings by constantly redefining that mystery. This may even lead formally to the formulation, as fresh statements, of further developments of the original statements, which remain materially the same.

If dogmatic theology is concerned with the whole of the Church's tradition, then we are bound to ask what it means for the word of Scripture to be preserved in conceptual, objective language which is neither that of Scripture nor that of contemporary man. Should we not be content simply to go back again and again to the Bible? Is it possible to do that? We have therefore to find a reason for the continued existence of dogmatic theology that will do full justice not only to the unique historical event of revelation in Christ, but also to the distance in time between modern man and that event.

In this, we should not forget that the biblical "statement" is not simply the primitive preliminary outline of the later dogmatic statements, something which is only of interest to us nowadays because it is the original statement to which we are committed. Or would it be more true to say that this biblical statement has been superseded, surpassed and rendered superfluous by the later dogmatic statements?

Many manuals of dogmatic theology give this impression. But how can the theologian who is concerned with the validity of Scripture prove that he is so concerned? He may insist that dogmatic definitions, with the classic metaphysical structure, always have to be supplemented by scriptural statements with their

[7] H. Schlier, "Biblische und dogmatische Theologie", in L. Klein, ed., *Diskussion über die Bibel* (Mainz, ²1964), p. 94.

living orientation towards man's salvation. The dogmatic theologian's reply to this would simply be that dogmatic theology could achieve this result as soon as those who practise it learn how to speak in dynamic, non-conceptual language. The scriptural scholar might further object to the idea of dogmatic theology fulfilling this function of continuing to express scriptural statements because it deals with so few biblical texts—mainly those which can be translated as directly as possible and without much reference to the context into the language of metaphysics. The obvious reply to this is that it is simply not so. Finally, there is the very important question as to whether it is possible for the systematic theologian to do sufficient justice to the great multiplicity of theological aspects in Scripture. This multiplicity, however, is a datum which has to be considered here in greater detail, because it is the hinge on which the relationship between exegesis and dogmatic theology ultimately turns. The problem of this relationship is best approached, I believe, from the standpoint of exegesis.

III. The Exegetical Problem

Very often in dogmatic theology, one New Testament author has been consulted almost exclusively in connection with a particular question, even though it might have been possible to resort to others. For instance, early christology relied almost entirely on John, the Catholic notion of the apostles has been predominantly based on Acts, and the Protestant doctrine of justification leans heavily on Paul. Stauffer, Meinertz and Bultmann, too, have not dealt at all with the synoptics, and have concentrated on Paul and John.[8] On the other hand, the Enlightenment led to a great interest in the synoptics and especially in Mark, but this was the result of a reaction against dogmatism, which was carried over into the theological interpretation of these gospels. Research into the history of editing during the last few decades, however, has proved the existence of an autonomous

[8] H. Schlier, "Über Sinn und Aufgabe einer Theologie des Neuen Testaments", in H. Vorgrimler, *Exegese und Dogmatik, op. cit.*, pp. 69–90, esp. p. 78.

theology in the synoptic gospels, because the differences between the gospels and the very divergent selection of traditional material can to a great extent be explained in the light of the different theological ideas contained in the gospels. The multiplicity of New Testament statements, often very difficult to reconcile with each other, is not based exclusively on different sources or author-ship, but above all on different theological ideas.

One important question is whether a text originated in the early days of the Church, when Christians were still expecting the Lord's imminent return, or towards the end of the first cen-tury, when they were prepared for a long period of waiting. But the differences cannot always be understood as different stages in a homogeneous development. They are often of such different kinds that they cannot simply be classified under one dogmatic system. All the different New Testament authors—the Jew from Jerusalem, the Jew from the diaspora, and the Greek Christian—came to their task with different theological points of view.

Is it possible, then, to speak of one scriptural testimony in the light of such multiplicity? Käsemann thinks not: "The diver-sity of the New Testament kerygma demonstrates that there were many different confessions in primitive Christianity exist-ing side by side, following each other, combining with each other and separating themselves from each other. All these con-fessions appealed, quite understandably, to the New Testament canon, and the exegete cannot deny them the objective right to do so. Regarding the whole canon as binding, these various con-fessions naturally claimed for themselves well-known or less well-known New Testament authors, and greater or lesser parts of Scripture, and did so with well-founded or less well-founded historical right. Their claim is fundamentally incontestable and can be proved. Both the unity of the Church, on the other hand, and any claim on the part of one confession to be absolute, are contestable and cannot be proved. Is Lessing's story of the three rings in his play *Nathan der Weise* to be the last word here? I think that it would be if the only task of the exegete were to establish historical facts. The biblical scholar who bases all his research on 'it is written . . .' is bound, in my opinion, to conclude that all critical study of the New Testament must end with an acknowledgment of Lessing's fable."[9]

It is possible to show that in detailed exegesis there is also a great deal of agreement between the different confessions. Nowadays, there is, generally speaking, controversy only about what the texts say to us, not about what they say objectively. As far as the validity and justification of the canon is concerned, there is once again general agreement that it includes those texts which are in a special way the literary deposit of the apostolic proclamation. The question, then, is whether it can, in view of the multiplicity of its texts, really be a binding norm. Can this multiplicity be interpreted differently, as Käsemann believes? Can these many different Scriptures really be, in spite of their multiplicity, the true development of a joint testimony to a content that is common to all the Scriptures and to a word of God proclaimed to man with ultimately only *one* meaning? Schlier thinks that it can, maintaining that the kerygma, as the normative apostolic *paradosis*, preceded the Gospel as a proclamation not only in time, but also with regard to content.[10]

Schlier justifies his interpretation of this plurality of texts by saying that it is only a multiplicity of beginnings, or of very fragmentary theologies, so that all that has to be done is to extend these many different theological lines until they come together again. In this way, the New Testament canon can be understood as the framework within which the various interpretations of this kerygma are valid and therefore binding. This does not mean that there is no objective centre to Scripture. This centre is Jesus Christ or justification through Jesus Christ, in so far as all that is meant by this is that the revelation of Jesus Christ has as its aim the salvation of mankind.

In this sense, then, the canon has a centre and a periphery. Many of the Scriptures had to wait for a long time before they were recognized as canonical, and different Churches include different Scriptures in their canons. Viewed as a whole, however,

---

[9] E. Käsemann, "Begründet der neutestamentliche Kanon die Einheit der Kirche?", *op. cit.*, p. 221.

[10] H. Schlier, "Kerygma und Sophia.—Zur neutestamentlichen Grundlegung des Dogmas", in *Die Zeit der Kirche* (Freiburg, 1956), pp. 206–32, esp. p. 216.

these differences are not important, and the canon remains the positive norm by which any genuine interpretation can determine its limits. In so far as they relate to realities within the New Testament, terms like "Palestinian", "Hellenistic", "primitive Church" and "early Catholic" are not *value judgments*. Because it forms part of the canon, a New Testament scripture can be regarded as just as binding as the Church as such. This essentially Catholic idea thus refers back, not as an exegetical justification of the canon, but as an ecclesiological basis for it, to dogmatic theology.

If this ecclesiological conception is not acceptable, the canon may bear witness to a community that has *mis*understood Scripture.[11] This, of course, gives rise to the need for a purely exegetical criterion for the interpretation of Scripture. Several attempts have been made to solve this problem.

Some scholars have tried to discover the original sources in the traditional testimonies, but this process has raised a number of difficult questions. Is this course possible, in view of the existing data? If it is only possible to some degree, can this limited fragment be accepted as a valid criterion? Can we distinguish between the scriptural statement and the historical event to such an extent that the latter is not clear as a testimony and the ability of the former to determine the life history of man and therefore to make him adopt a certain attitude is also obscured? Or does a distinction of this kind not imply that it is impossible for God to act in the world? A deeper insight into the reality of the divine word is clearly required here.

This is why E. Käsemann calls for a criticism of the *content*— the essential matter of the message—rather than an historical criticism.[12] Scripture has to be understood, he insists, primarily in the light of the content of the message, of which it is the literary record. This message, this "gospel" is the "critical authority against which Scripture is measured".[13] This is, according to

---

[11] E. Käsemann, "Begründet der neutestamentliche Kanon die Einheit der Kirche?", *op. cit.*, p. 220.

[12] E. Käsemann, "Neutestamentliche Fragen von heute", *ZTK* (1957), pp. 1–21, esp. p. 9.

[13] E. Käsemann, "Zum Thema der Nichtobjektivierbarkeit", in *Exegetische Versuche und Besinnungen*, I, pp. 224-36, 230.

Käsemann, the basis of the Protestant position. But this claim also raises a number of questions. What is the criterion for the degree to which Scripture bears witness to this "gospel"? Will the scholar not take as his criterion the interpretation of one New Testament author (such as Paul), which is the testimony of *his special*—and purely fortuitous—history, and measure the validity of other interpretations against it? When Käsemann says that "the sum total of all the individual scriptural testimonies is not the Gospel",[14] can I reach this "gospel" by a process of subtraction, or should I renounce every external criterion and make my own subjective involvement my criterion? Certainly, the scholar who entrusts himself to this movement as proof of the power of the word of God will soon find himself in a vicious circle.

It is not really possible to accuse the Catholic theologian, with his conviction of the binding force of the New Testament canon, of an unseemly longing for security. What is at the root of this conviction is faith that God will see to it that his definitive word has in fact come and will come again. The Church, whose origin is in the canon, is more than a guardian of the truth. It is the community of those who are joined through faith to the one Lord and to each other. Should I not, precisely for this reason, attribute to the Church the promised Spirit who will lead it into all truth? Of course, this Spirit must also cleanse the heart of every believer so that he can see the truth with the eyes of faith. But the individual believer is not simply committed to his own individual experience of faith—he is also always exposed to sin, which obstructs the truth. This at once raises the question as to whether this interpretation of kerygmatic statements can lead, when the person interpreting them has abandoned all external criteria, to a possible correction of his prior understanding. Or is this prior understanding not made the exclusive norm for interpretation, and is the statement of the evangelist not acknowledged in advance to be the kerygma only when this statement can be interpreted on the basis of this prior understanding? Surely this would simply be a modern form of gnosticism?

I have done no more than indicate a few of the many questions that are raised in connection with the relationship between

[14] E. Käsemann, "Neutestamentliche Fragen von heute", *op. cit.*, p. 9.

exegesis and dogmatic theology, and a few of the authors who have already entered into dialogue with each other. So many questions remain unanswered that this dialogue, based on respect for the subject and for each other, must continue. Its aim should above all be to ensure that God's word remains God's word, and at the same time a living word.

Translated by David Smith

Luis Alonso Schökel

Is Exegesis Necessary?

IS scientific exegesis necessary, or does the Church possess a prior, broader understanding of Scripture than that provided by exegesis? This understanding would be one common to all Christians, of Scripture as the word of God, of its dimension as message and summons. It would be the broader field within which formal inquiry of a scientific nature would take place. This would seem to indicate that scientific exegesis needs this first, common understanding—which, however, has no need of exegesis.

I. Some Examples

Examples that any professional exegete who takes on pastoral duties can have come across will illustrate the abstract question posed above. Let us take first the case of the Christian of little education who does not understand the first (OT) reading of the Mass; then the case of the Christian with some education who decides to read the Old Testament for himself and gives up when he reaches Leviticus. In the course of lecturing to the clergy on the Old Testament, I have more than once heard this comment: "All this is very interesting, but it means that one has to be a professional exegete in order to understand the Old Testament." At the other end of the scale is the Christian in the habit of reading certain books of the Bible with interest and profit, who finds that when he starts looking for scientific explanations that the simple has become complicated, and the familiar abstruse.

Is the Bible a book for specialists, or does one have to do without the specialists in order to understand the Bible?

Let us take a few biblical examples. First, there is the famous one of the eunuch minister of Queen Candace of the Ethiopians (Acts 8. 27–39), who cannot understand the text of Isaiah unless someone explains it to him. In fact this example is of limited value, since the eunuch understands the words well enough (the meaning), and is ignorant only of whom they refer to (the application).

In Ezek. 3, a chapter outlining the activity of the prophets, God speaks to his prophet in these words: "Son of man, go, get you to the house of Israel, and speak with my words to them. For you are not sent to a people of foreign speech and a hard language. . . . Surely, if I sent you to such, they would listen to you. But the house of Israel will not listen to you; for they are not willing to listen to me." That is to say, the message and the words are clear, even for people who speak another language; what stands in the way of understanding is the wrong disposition of the Israelites. Ezekiel is, after all, speaking to them about their own problems, in their own language, and does not need an interpreter to make himself understood.

This second example does not prove much either. Firstly, we are not the prophet's original audience, and our problems are not the same as those of the Israelites. Secondly, Ezekiel's own immediate and later disciples felt obliged to explain and apply the prophet's words in order to make them comprehensible to succeeding generations.

Ezekiel's countrymen went to listen to him as they would to an "amorous ballad-monger", because they did not want to listen to the word of God. We do want to listen to the word of God, but we lack the key to its language. I believe that today most people would say that they do not understand the Scriptures unless an expert explains them to them.

II. The Problem in Universal Terms

The problem of scientific exegesis is usually posed in terms of different levels: the specialist, the pastor and the simple faithful. In this way it can be discussed without going beyond the confines of a single society. But I believe it can only be seen in its full extent when it is posed in universal terms.

Scientific exegesis is a Western product today; indeed, when it comes to the Old Testament, it is not merely Western, but almost exclusively German and Anglo-American. So it is no use talking about some abstract, hypothetical exegesis; one has to take the one in existence; and so the question today has to be posed in these terms: "Does a Chinaman need German scientific exegesis to understand Scripture? Does an African need Anglo-American exegetical knowledge?" These are cultural extremes, but one can pursue this line and ask whether the Christians of Latin America need specialists from the United States to teach them the word of God, and how far the more or less Catholic countries of the Mediterranean need the wonders of German exegesis.

These questions do not spring from any nationalistic or polemical intentions; on the contrary, they are designed to denounce the danger of cultural nationalism being applied to no less a matter than the word of God. This brings me to a criticism of modern scientific exegesis, in regard to which I propose to concentrate on the Old Testament, which is my own specialism and the most inaccessible part of Scripture for most Christians.

III. Criticism of Scientific Exegesis

The layman, and the specialist too, finds an enormous complexity in today's biblical science; so many auxiliary disciplines, additional inquiries and differentiated techniques seem to be required. Can this complexity really be imposed by the biblical text (they might ask), or does it come largely from the type of problems that exegetes set themselves? Both the layman and the initiate can be surprised to find themselves suspecting, at the back of their minds, that all the problems that professional exegetes set themselves are not really of any relevance or importance for an understanding of Scripture, but are rather the initiation rites for a very exclusive club. Are they not all really insoluble problems, whose continued airing serves merely to give a semblance of activity to a number of really idle people?

Such suspicions can only be confirmed by the disconcerting

plurality of opinions on a whole variety of biblical texts, a plurality that does not seem to be acceptable, but composed of mutually exclusive hypotheses. What or whom should the layman pay attention to?

Then exegetes have developed their own particular language. When the translation of a German series into Spanish was being planned, it proved necessary to draw up a list of two thousand special terms used in Old Testament exegesis, and to fix a translation for each of them in advance. Does such a terminological barricade help to actualize the Bible, to make it accessible to Christians all over the world today? Or is it just a defensive wall around the privileged city of the specialists? (And this merely in regard to terminology, not to mention the crushing weight of erudition that commentaries also impose on the layman.)

So the gravamen of this critical look seems to be negative. Biblical science today is more of a hindrance than a help to an understanding of the Scriptures. If one draws this conclusion, one can easily be led into the familiar demand for a return to the simple life, to the freshness of personal and immediate understanding, rooted in the experience of life itself. For some, this means removing the elaborate structure they have built up, freeing themselves from it; for others, remaining in the blessed state of simplicity they are still in, and defending themselves from complications.

IV. THE BENEFITS OF SCIENTIFIC EXEGESIS

While recognizing the strength of the preceding criticisms— which could easily be extended and made harsher—it must be stated that the mere denial of scientific exegesis neither solves nor eliminates the problem. The individual cannot take refuge in his personal experience to read the Bible in the light of his own tastes and inspiration. The Bible is essentially a social document, the book of a people for a people, and the problems of its reading and interpretation can only be worked out within the community.

So the question remains: now we have to ask if scientific exegesis can provide a service to the universal community and the local communities of the Church, and then whether this service is necessary.

(a) *Service of Translation.* The average Christian reads the Bible in translation. Translating means transposing a text from one linguistic system to another, and a linguistic system is a complex structure embracing far more than grammar and vocabulary.

The translator, faced with his starting-point, the Hebrew and Greek of the Old and New Testaments, makes use of an enormous amount of specialized knowledge and techniques, and exercises a variety of exegetical options without explicitly rationalizing each choice or mentioning the possible alternatives he has excluded.

The average Christian, opening his Bible in search of the word of God, is taking advantage, although he does not realize it, of the results of thousands, perhaps millions, of hours of work, work done by hundreds, perhaps thousands of specialists. Many pericopes, even phrases, have been established as the result of a century of joint investigation, and while there may be only one translator, he never works in a vacuum.

This service of translation is indispensable, and will go on perpetually in every country in every age. Translating is the first and primary means of actualizing a word that only remains itself in its constant transformation into different languages.

(b) *Linguistic Service.* It is quite possible for people to start to read the Bible in their own language, and give up because they do not understand it. This is a linguistic problem, distinct from the problem of translation.

It is true that extensive and regular reading of the Bible brings familiarity with the linguistic problems posed, but this in itself is insufficient, being very slow, and liable to leave ample room for misunderstandings. The professional exegete has a most important role here too.

The service he can render may be summarized under four heads: concepts, symbols, formulas and structures. The explanation of these elements can be given either systematically, or as notes to the text. Biblical concepts and their evolution within their linguistic field, by comparison with their likes or opposites, will be studied systematically: in a biblical dictionary, for example. Biblical symbols are less extensively treated in such works, largely because biblical knowledge is very backward in this field. But the specialist can identify and group related symbols, show their human origin, and suggest lines for further thought. Biblical formulas have now largely been identified and classified, as typical of a particular genre, tendency or author, but as yet they have not been systematically listed; they are indicated in commentaries accompanying the text. Structures are extremely important, being repeated and varied throughout the Bible: knowledge of them enables the reader to grasp the different unities organically, to perceive the often theological relationships between their different elements; it also enables him to transpose the biblical structure into present-day situations, in which the component parts will be different but the structure the same. Biblical language is shown in this way to have both unity and generative force.

The layman would have difficulty in discovering all these aspects of the shaping and realization of the biblical message for himself. The specialist must necessarily be the explorer in these fields, putting the benefits of his discoveries at the service of the community. It is his exploratory function that is paramount; his discoveries can be passed on either directly by him, or through intermediaries.

(c) The specialist also offers the community the *rigour* of his training and methods. With this, he can change the immediate understanding of the faithful into controlled understanding, can criticize unwarranted interpretations, and measure the probability of opinions. Christians who belong to critical, scientific cultures cannot renounce the use of this acquired knowledge.

(d) Finally, new scientific methods can reveal hidden riches in a biblical text that would not otherwise be apparent, even to an attentive reader. I am thinking of, for example, the theological advance brought by the technical analysis of the composition of the gospels (German *Redaktionsgeschichte*): this is like a rebirth of the old treatise *"De mysteriis vitae Christi"* broken down into the theologies of the various evangelists.

To sum up, one can say that scientific exegesis deals with a series of problems that have universal and permanent validity: those of translation and linguistic structure, for example. It also deals with questions whose interest is limited in space and time. The distinction may be banal, but it has considerable practical application, in that the export of local problems can be useless and even harmful.

V. TRADITION

The service we have discussed also applies to the community application, so that the body of specialized exegetes has a duty to share its common understanding of Scripture as the word of God with the Christian community. This is where the concept of tradition comes in, not as an alternative opposed to scientific exegesis, but as a sort of ambit within which exegesis unfolds its critical function in a dialectical movement.

If one understands tradition in the Vatican II sense of being above all real tradition, then Scripture becomes part of the reality handed down, incorporated into the total life of the Church, and bound to the differing aspects of Christian experience. Within this tradition, Scripture is less theoretical and more experiential, subject more to "criticism by the spirit" than to scientific criticism, less individualistic and more communitarian; it is also partially detached from its original context to assimilate itself to the new existential context, and is more amenable to contemplation than to investigation.

In the liturgy and para-liturgical services, biblical pericopes are chosen, and Old Testament readings are combined with psalms and New Testament passages so as to bring out relationships between them; the homily comments on these texts, and the eucharistic rite give them a centre; the texts unfold throughout a liturgical year that re-enacts the culminating points of the history of salvation.

All this is the process of tradition handing on and interpreting the Scriptures: the average Christian draws his spiritual nourishment from this process, and so should the professional exegete. But at a time in history such as ours, one cannot simply say that the whole of this process precedes all scientific exegesis, since these selections and combinations as well as translations and homilies, all exploit the results of technical analysis. What has been said of the liturgy applies also, in differing degrees, to catechesis and spirituality.

The Church's tradition has an incredible capacity for selecting, assimilating and giving life to the most significant discoveries of earlier ages, whether they are the fruit of contemplation or of study. Christians may well receive and assimilate biblical teaching through a homily that quotes St Augustine, or from reading Thomas à Kempis. This mediated access to Scripture is not to be despised, though it now seems insufficient to us. But even Thomas à Kempis, with all his aversion to *"lectio scholastica"* in favour of *"lectio monastica"*, could not do without the legacy of exegetical science down to his day.

VI. TRADITIONS

Should the treasures accumulated in one tradition, fed by the exegetical science of the past, be considered sufficient?

Not at all. At each moment of history, tradition should engage in a critical dialogue with the current exegetical science of each age and each region. The flood of the main tradition still carries the tributaries of other traditions. Sometimes these dry up, and then there is no point in trying to keep them artificially flowing; others may cut themselves off from the main stream to the point where they give rise to deviant and unacceptable traditions. An example of this would be the legitimate vision of Christian allegory degenerating into petty allegorism. There are also partial interpretations, which show their limitations when set in an organic context, as happened to the unilaterally "spiritualistic" tradition. Sometimes ignorance of the historical context gives a text an absolute value it does not in fact possess; once reset in its historical context, the text reveals its conditioning factors and loses its rigidity.

Scientific exegesis today has a function in criticizing the multiplicity of traditions which have grown up without sufficient discipline or accountability. This means that it is not now sufficient to appeal to tradition for an understanding of Scripture, because one may be appealing to human traditions or customs. Not only did Christ denounce those who set aside the commandments of God "because of their traditions"; the Old Testament also contains similar warnings: Isa. 29. 13, "their fear of me is a commandment of men learned by rote"; Ezek. 20. 18, 19, "Do not walk in the statutes of your fathers... walk in my statutes".

*   *   *

The problem of scientific exegesis and the common understanding of Scripture should be posed with "catholic" breadth, taking the different types of culture proper to different communities into account. The problem should be posed and resolved only in communitarian terms. The problem cannot be resolved by eliminating one of its factors. The solution begins to appear when the interdependence of both factors is recognized.

Scientific exegesis is justified if it can offer a necessary or useful service to the ecclesial community, and to the degree that this service is necessary or useful.

Scientific exegesis can deal with questions conditioned by the tastes of the age or region, but must avoid the dangers of concentrating on irrelevant problems, of gratuitously complicating what is simple, and of replacing deep understanding with erudition. It will be able to avoid these dangers only by keeping in contact with Christian experience and retaining a living understanding of Scripture.

Tradition also transmits Scripture and interprets it in a living context; one of the ways it does this is to make use of discoveries of scientific exegesis.

Tradition can, however, include traditions that hinder a right understanding of Scripture today.

Translated by Paul Burns

Gotthold Hasenhüttl

Dialogue between the Dogmatic Theologian and the Exegete

I. The Basic Principle of Dogmatic Theology: Dialogue
with the Exegete

EVERY science is conditioned by its basic principles, and its truth
is decided by the credibility of its grounds. Accordingly, every
aspect of dogmatic theology is dependent on exegesis. Even
though no dogmatic theologian would wish to convict the Bible
of error on dogmatic grounds, it has often enough tried to function as a guideline for exegesis; it did not engage in dialogue
with exegetes, but adopted the authoritarian ploy of *requiring*
an exegesis to be carried out; what was believed "explicitly"
must not appear "implicitly" in Scripture. In this way, theology
succeeded in reducing exegesis to a helpless state which brought
its seriousness under question. By "subduing" exegesis, dogmatic
theology severed a vital root. By viewing exegetes as mere "sup-
pliers" of its raw material, dogmatic theology did not take its
given basis seriously, and in fact undermined its own foundations. By attacking Scripture prematurely, without attending to
the critically revisionist exegetes, it devalued the text, and thus
itself.

The basic presumption is a destruction of the text by using it
as *"dictum probantum"*—as evidence. In this pre-critical and
naïve stage of dogmatics, the Bible was used as a quarry for
enhancing the lustre of a dogmatic thesis. The root and starting-
point of a thesis is not a factually-grounded interpretation by
objectively critical exegetes, and therefore not the text understood properly, but the theological thesis. The latter takes the

place of the text as a text to be understood. In this self-sufficiency, dogmatics rejects the Bible as a basis.[1] Hence the poverty of so many dogmatic assertions. But if dogmatics is a realization of faith oriented to self-comprehension and explanation, it can exist only in a dialogue with Scripture made possible by the exegete. *"Te totum applica ad textum: rem totam applica ad te."*[2] This is not a biblicistic requirement, which holds the expression of faith developed in the course of history to be a false one, but the primary requirements that dogmatics does not stand in its own way, but instead remains open to the Bible, in which God's word is to be heard.

If the dogmatic thesis is merely garnished with biblical citations, the dialogue is broken off, and exegesis (the decisive corrective of dogmatic theology) is excluded. Karl Barth deserves unqualified assent when he claims that exegesis is the sole criterion for all dogmatic propositions, so that every point in the Creed that cannot be demonstrated exegetically has to be struck out.[3] Dogmatics is powerless, however, being without "God's aid", if it uses exegesis as a support for its system without attending to objective criticism.

Today, after Vatican II, dogmatics appears—theoretically at least—to conform to this requirement. For, in the Decree on Priestly Formation (art. 16), we read: "Dogmatic theology should be so arranged that the biblical themes are presented first"; only then should the history of dogma and its relation to the general history of the Church be taken into account. This is not a question of a purely external arrangement, but of a fundamental reliance on exegesis. In the Dogmatic Constitution on Divine Revelation (art. 12) this is brought out even more emphatically: "It is the task of exegetes to work ... towards a better understanding and explanation of the meaning of sacred Scripture, so that through preparatory study the judgment of the Church may mature." The Church and dogmatic theology are

---

[1] Cf. B. van Iersel, "Interpretation von Schrift und Dogma", in *Die Interpretation des Dogmas* (ed. P. Schoonenberg; Düsseldorf, 1969), pp. 38 ff.

[2] J. A. Bengel, Preface to a pocket edition of the Greek New Testament, 1734.

[3] Cf. K. Barth, *Credo* (Munich, 1935), pp. 153 ff.

therefore essentially oriented by exegesis; without exegesis there is no mature judgment but only arbitrary prejudice. Hence the dogmatic theologian is required to engage in dialogue with the exegete. However, he is often let down by the exegete. If the exegete allows himself to be degraded to the condition of an auxiliary scholar, he cannot help the dogmatic theologian. When he allowed himself to be muzzled by the decrees of the Biblical Commission, he was partly responsible for the inadequacies of theology.

This misunderstanding, which made dialogue impossible on both sides, led to the great diastasis, for exegesis liberated itself and went its own way.

II. Exegesis within the Church

The form-historical method, historico-critical research as a whole, and so on, saw themselves as external to any ecclesiastico-dogmatic pronouncements, which were no longer taken into account. Hence Karl Rahner can say to the exegete: "...you exegetes forget sometimes that you are Catholic theologians... that you are engaged in a subject which is an integral part of Catholic theology as a whole and which must, therefore, observe all those principles which are in fact proper to Catholic theology. For this reason, Catholic exegesis is a science of faith and not merely a science of language and of religion; there exists a positive relationship between your science and the faith... of the Church."[4] Karl Barth made a similar demand: "Exegesis, which so to speak precedes dogmatic theology, has to be an attempt to understand sacred Scripture within the Church, and must therefore be *theological* exegesis."[5] Exegesis alienated itself by shunning the parish. Its suppression by dogmatic theology brought about its exodus. This made dialogue all the more difficult to contemplate. Dogmatic theology, deprived of any assistance, became even more incapable of development. The new exegesis was placed over against the old dogmatics; and even today this makes a genuine rapprochement difficult though not impossible. Only if exegesis

---

[4] Karl Rahner, *Theological Investigations*, Vol. V (London, 1966), p. 70.
[5] K. Barth, *op. cit.*, p. 153.

is constantly present within the Christian community as a potentially explosive material can the dogmatic element in the understanding of revelation be urged forward.

Neither the forceful suppression and appropriation of exegesis by dogmatic theology, nor its flight from "slavery" into the area of an alienated freedom, can help the dogmatic theologian in any way and contribute anything to his own development. Instead, exegesis must challenge dogmatic theology to debate, and in such a way that it perceives its proper critical function. "Biblical theology has . . . a critical function apart from this dogmatic theology . . . and the actual proclamation of faith in each case; and this applies however small the extent to which dogmatics and proclamation can be determined solely from the basis of biblical theology. The *real* starting-point of the kerygma of faith (which rests in Scripture), although still a starting-point, always remains the greater and more comprehensive element which makes possible and controls progress."[6]

Accordingly the exegete is not called upon to create harmony by a process of simplification, but to make the distinction clear and to criticize from the basis of the biblical witness. When exegesis is exercised confidently within the community, it acknowledges its duty as "critical negativity". Since dogmatic theology must always be systematic, and attempt to posit absolutely the particular system and institution that result in practice, the exegete has to try, on the basis of Scripture (unsystematic and always more profound), to exert an anti-systematic effect and to relativize the institution. Only in this way can dogmatic theology be urged forward, unfold, revise itself, and move on towards the new.

III. The Exegete as a Helper

But this basic alienation of the two disciplines is not the only source of misunderstanding. The modes of expression are also at fault. The language of each often uses the same words for quite different concepts. We only have to think of terms such as

[6] Karl Rahner, "Biblische Theologie und Dogmatik in ihrem wechselseitigen Verhältnis", *LThK*, 11, p. 451; see also H. Petri, *Exegese und Dogmatik* (Paderborn, 1966), pp. 236 ff.

"flesh" or "grace" to see this. For example, a clear indication of which notion of grace is really intended in Scripture would be extremely valuable for dogmatic theology. The exegete should develop a critical position in regard to the basic dogmatic terms on the basis of his analyses of biblical vocabulary. He should also take decisive dogmatic concepts as guidelines for, and focal points of, his exegesis. On the other hand, biblical concepts which are alien to dogmatic theology should be systematically limited. All the way from the notion of God to the "last things" there is room for a conceptual tightening-up which would be of value to dogmatic theologians and exegetes alike.

But this process of dialogue should not be restricted to concepts. Objective and critical insight into the development of sacred Scripture is extremely useful, and could become a model for study of the development of dogmas. Unfortunately objective criticism is still an alien notion as far as dogmatic theology is concerned. It is alleged that many exegetes attribute error to the Bible as a result of objective criticism. But if Scripture is taken quite seriously as human discourse, error is a definite possibility. For instance, there is surely an error in Mk. 9. 1, which speaks of those "who will not taste death". Did Jesus really never make a mistake? Wouldn't the capability of error bring him closer to us as a man? And don't these considerations apply to dogmatic statements as well? Objective criticism would allow us to look in a new and more analytic way at the historicity of ecclesiastical practice and dogmas. But of course the help that exegesis could give in this respect won't come through a simple, straightforward exegesis of dogmas.

Holy Writ cannot be written anew; but the fixed form of expression can be subjected to new interpretations. Dogmas, however, require new formulations, precisely because they represent not only part of the Bible which demands up-to-date translation, but are also of their nature manifestations of the living and genuine development of faith. Therefore, whereas Scripture to a certain extent has an unlimited validity for the Christian, this is not true of dogmas, which have to be reformulated. Here, too, exegesis must be clear about its function, so that the linguistic adjustments carried out arise from a process of dialogue with

Scripture and make the faith comprehensible for the modern Christian.

The exegete can have a liberating effect in revealing untenable dogmatic biblical authorities. For example, Aquinas's suggestion that a number of the sacraments are not mentioned in the Bible for arcane disciplinary reasons is an artificial form of "exegesis" used to save the face of dogmatic pronouncements. Similarly, the exegete has to risk saying unequivocally whether anything like original sin, angels, devils, and so on, really is postulated in the Bible, and whether Mt. 16. 18 is a seriously authoritative text. Then exegesis would offer an invaluable critique of tradition, which would also be able to show the legitimacy or illegitimacy of new concepts and assertions (e.g., the *homoousios,* infallibility, and so on). The exegete should concern himself with themes such as the present-day understanding of property in the Church, so that he can offer a biblio-theological picture of the concept of property held by the first Christians. This would not mean an unhistorical representation of old sociological conditions, but a corrective that would probably stop certain social theories being palmed off as "Christian". The same applies to pre-marital intercourse, the indissolubility of marriage, the arrangements of institutional law, and so on. Then, perhaps, some dogmatic prejudice, and some unobjective and inexpert exegetical "amens" (reinforcement) would undergo a relativization that would correspond more to man as he is actually called by God.

IV. Refusing Help

However, exegesis can do all this only if it is not restricted to editorial history, historical criticism, form-history, and so on, but interprets existentially, or—to put it negatively—when it "demythologizes" within the community of the Church, and for its sake. The conversion of detailed exegesis of phraseology and contexts into a form *to be understood now* is an indispensable aid to dogmatic theology. But the exegete can do this only if he takes the philosophical self-understanding of contemporary man into account, which is a source, too, for the dogmatic theologian. In this way, by reason of the dialogic structure of truth,[7] the

[7] See G. Hasenhüttl, *Füreinander dasein* (Freiburg, 1971), pp. 12 ff.

word of God could be heard *in* the word of man. The exegete's assistance can nevertheless be refused in a number of ways: some have already been mentioned. Wherever allegorization, the *sensus plenior*, and so on, are offered as substitutes for objective criticism, exegesis does not help but only inhibits dogmatic theology. Some exegetes have often been less careful than Aquinas, who asserted that any sense of a biblical text must correspond to the sense of the words as the author intended them.[8] To assume a meaning that was not humanly mediated would mean asserting that God's revelation was unhistorical.

Another way for the exegete to escape his historical liability is recourse to purely historico-critical considerations which prevent any position being taken up in regard to problems of the present moment. This form of exegesis is wont to cite an allegedly higher "pure science" which is free from any particular interest, in contradistinction to mere "fashionable tendencies". Retreat into the indefinite and vague is of little use. A refusal to establish hypotheses is inimical to the potentialities of biblical science. Even the old-style attempts to harmonize OT and NT, one Old Testament author and another, NT and tradition, are of no help. Or there is the emphasis on the uniqueness of the text, which is usually represented by apologetic interests and tends to cancel any objective view. Or very often the pattern is implicitly and explicitly no more than sleight of hand to justify the *status quo*. Something is understood more "deeply" and "precisely" only if the context can really be logically demonstrated. Otherwise it is better openly to admit the "unknown quantity", which need not prejudice the value and truth of the assertion.

The above-mentioned arbitrarily selected questions addressed to the exegete can be added to almost at will. The dialogue between exegesis and dogmatic theology is indispensable for both of them. Both have to try to trace the connecting lines and indicate their requirements. I think it would be impossible to link them rigidly, as is often suggested, for only a dynamic interaction through dialogue can prove fruitful. If exegesis refuses its critical function in this dialogue, the interaction will be cut

---

[8] St Thomas Aquinas, *Summa Th.* I *a.* 10 *ad* 1: "... *omnes sensus fundentur super unum, scilicet litteralem; ex quo solo potest trahi argentum, non autem ex iis quae secundum allegoriam dicuntur.*"

short. But when its help is not rejected, and neither party strives for dominion over the other, nor seeks to retire from the fray, dogmatic theology will be able to live up to its premisses and exegesis will accede to a reality that will urge the dogmatic theologian forward, so that both bear witness to God's word in the word of man.

Translated by John Griffiths

Meinrad Limbeck

The Exegete's Answer

I. The Basic Principle of Dogmatic Theology

THERE is hardly an idea in the area of systematic theology that the exegete would accept more readily and unconditionally than the requirement that modern exegetical findings should be accorded full rights and included in contemporary theology. In this belief, it is led on neither by a covert need for recognition nor by a romantic attitude toward the origins which can believe in the working of the Spirit only at the very start, and too easily assesses all later developments as deviation and decadence. Even though much in the systematic theological debate concerns the exegete and his science, this is largely because his acquaintance with the New Testament has shown him the variety (and also a certain relativity) of the original theological attempts to interpret the divine salvific action which occurred in Jesus Christ.

For this reason, sacred Scripture itself is a source of a certain discontent, when he sees present-day theology almost too content with conventional formulas and theses, and hardly daring to translate the cause of God in Jesus Christ into a changed mode of thinking and talking. But, for this very reason, he is also convinced that those systematic theologians who take the variousness of articulations of the scriptural witness quite seriously, must attempt *new* interpretations of the Gospel, which—in regard to the Bible—could not be so easily accused of plain deviation from the true faith. For this reason, the exegete is especially grateful for those theologians whose work does not make him feel that they think the exegete's attempted interpretations are intended to deprive the Christian of the real value of his faith,[1] but instead emphasizes the variety of *possible* interpretations offered by exegesis.

Admittedly, even though exegesis today ought to be especially important for the further development of theology, there are two reasons for possible dangers if contemporary theology conducts its dialogue primarily with exegesis.

1. Even the New Testament texts are not simply the Gospel which the Church has to proclaim accessibly, but the initial, variously successful attempts to express anew the Gospel, that is, God's liberating message which was definitively made present to us in the person and activity of Jesus. Even though one cannot say that all these attempts are successful to the same extent, and even though their unacknowledged time-conditioned clothing on many occasions (and for a long time) made an appropriate understanding of individual words or passages impossible, nevertheless an enormous number of believers throughout the centuries were so affected by the spirit of these writings that *their* lives and thoughts represent a worthy interpretation and elucidation of the Gospel.[2] Therefore the exegete, who is concerned with the understanding *of the Gospel*, should regret any passing over or suppression within the whole Church of such interpretations of the Gospel, merely because on first inspection they appear to have been expressed in a language and in a conceptual world that do not accord with the nature of Scripture.

2. However different the individual documents of the New Testament may be, they all share the central concern of illuminating the "knowledge of the glory of God in the face of Christ" (2 Cor. 4. 5 f.), and do this in answer to very different questions, expectations and needs of partly still seeking, partly already believing men; hence not only revealed data and conceptual models

---

[1] Cf. J. Ratzinger, *Introduction to Christianity* (London, 1970).
[2] See H. Urs von Balthasar, "Theologie und Heiligkeit", *Verbum Caro* (Einsiedeln, 1960), pp. 195–225; E. Schillebeeckx, "Exegese, Dogmatik und Dogmenentwicklung", in *Exegese und Dogmatik*, ed. H. Vorgrimler (Mainz, 1962), pp. 91–114 (esp. 99–101).

were taken from the Old Testament.[3] That is: the primitive Christian proclamation was clearly ready, for the sake of the Gospel, not only to speak all tongues (1 Cor. 9. 19–23) but to tackle questions and expectations unpremeditated by any believer, in order to answer them in the light of Jesus Christ. If contemporary theology is to remain true to this basic broadness of mind in primitive Christian proclamation, it must always perform an act of genuine spiritual poverty in regard to the questions and needs, problems and expectations of the men of *this* time and *this* world, in order to answer them in the spirit of Jesus Christ; without, perhaps, being able at the decisive points—such as, for example, in the "establishment of moral pointers"[4]—to obtain the direct support of exegesis.

II. The Requirement: Exegesis within the Church

"The Church and its Gospel came before the book that is the Bible, and from the beginning the Bible was a book emanating from the Church, and a book for and in the Church."[5] The exegete who respects this fact (no longer questioned by anyone today) finds that the New Testament itself refers him in his work to the functional sphere of the Church. For this reason, of course, theology and the official Church would rather not have him in this sphere, when (in his estimation justifiably) he dares to tackle long-unquestioned pillars of the building of faith. Yet this is the very point where the major difficulties are to be expected in the future.

For example, no one will refute Schnackenburg when he says: "Even the exegete, who moves from a historico-exegetical examination of tradition to a theological interpretation of the claims of Jesus, will remain oriented by the belief in Christ of the early Church, and also keep in mind the teaching developed and

---

[3] On the different influences on, e.g., the formation of New Testament Christology, see R. Schnackenburg, "Christologie des neuen Testaments", *Mysterium Salutis*, III/1 (Einsiedeln, 1970), pp. 227–388.

[4] Cf. A. Auer, "Zehn Thesen über die Findung sittlicher Weisungen, *Theol. Quartalschrift*, 149 (1969), pp. 75–85.

[5] K. H. Schelke, *Das neue Testament* (Kevelaer, 1970), p. 30.

assured today in the form represented by the magisterium."[6] But if the exegete is compelled to record a unique parallel between the concern to establish the divinity of Jesus (cf. Mk. 3. 23; Mt. 12. 25 par.; Mk. 6. 52 f.; Mt. 14. 33; Mk. 10. 18; Mt. 19. 17; Mk. 13. 31 f.; Lk. 21. 33; and so on) and, however, the concern to pass over the humanity of Jesus (Mk. 6. 6; Mt. 13. 58 par.; Mk. 9. 36; Mt. 18. 2 par.; Mk. 10. 14; Mt. 19. 14 par.), and if this concern is comparable with the process recognizable in the Old Testament in which the sinfulness and humanity of the chosen one became increasingly inconceivable (cf. 2 Sam. 6. 11 f.: 1 Chr. 13. 13 f.; 15. 3; 2 Sam. 7. 13 f.: 1 Chr. 17. 13; 2 Sam. 24. 1: 1 Chr. 21. 1), until in the end the chosen one was always sinless and obedient to the law (cf. Gen. 12. 10–13. 1: Job 13. 10–15; Gen. 27. 20–23: Job 26. 17 f., and so on), but the sinner was repudiated by God (4 Esd. 7. 129–131),[7] and if (nevertheless) this theologically sequacious Old Testament experience of faith was also refuted by Jesus' unconditional *Yes* to even the sinner (Mk. 2. 13–17; Lk. 15), then a continuing place in the Church may simply be refused those exegetes who ask whether the increasing emphasis in the New Testament on the metaphysically comprehended, pre-existent divinity of Jesus does not feature a (humanly very understandable) misunderstanding of God, according to which the sign of God must be something extraordinary? Is it not necessary, consciously, and within the Church and its theology, to allow such questioning, especially in view of the contrary reference to the Spirit, who will lead the Church to the truth of Jesus (Jn. 14. 26; 16. 12–15), so long as nothing was asserted that would denigrate the specific nature of this Spirit (Lk. 4. 17–21; 2 Cor. 3. 17–4, 6)— in regard, too, to the reality which is disclosed and recognizable through him alone.

It is certainly possible to understand the pluralistic and fragmentary elements in New Testament theology as requiring "the many broken lines to be extended a little, and the divergent lines to be made to converge on a single point",[8] in order to arrive at a

---

[6] R. Schnackenburg, "Zur dogmatischen Auswertung des Neuen Testaments", in *Exegese und Dogmatik* (see note 2 above), pp. 115–33, 118.

[7] Cf. M. Limbeck, *Die Ordnung des Heils* (Düsseldorf, 1971).

[8] H. Schlier, "Biblische und dogmatische Theologie", *Besinnung auf das Neue Testament* (Freiburg, 1967), pp. 25–34, 30.

definitive, binding total picture of the New Testament writings. But it is just as possible to detect within these writings attacks on others (for example, on the Jews, above all in John, but more certainly on Jewish-Christian circles in Paul) in these documents, together with an inability of individual writers really to understand their opponents and thus to enter into proficient dialogue with them. (For instance, the pious Jew must have seen himself as wholly misunderstood in the Pauline legal polemics.)

Even though such distortions and unjust judgments can be understood in terms of the historical situation of the various primitive Christian communities, they can hardly be asserted to be the effect of the Spirit of Jesus; nevertheless the influence of this attitude, with its incapacity for dialogue, on the structure of the New Testament writings is undeniable. Therefore we are obliged to ask to what extent "assertions which accord with sacred Scripture" allow the "glory of God in the face of Christ" to appear, and thus can and indeed must be decisive for the proclamation of the Gospel.

Certainly exegesis can no longer answer this question by itself. But systematic theology, too, is still far from being able to offer a convincing answer in this regard. And yet this answer would be a decisive prerequisite for making the possibilities and findings of historico-critical exegesis now available really fruitful for the Church, and for ensuring that the exegete and the questions which he *has to* pose are not referred away from the Church for an answer.

III. Ways in which the Exegete can help

Without doubt "exegesis as the *ancilla theologiae*" (A. Vögtle) will (of its own account) also seek dialogue with systematic theology; for "dogmatic theology legitimately poses . . . questions for biblical theology, which biblical theology cannot itself pose, and which nevertheless serve to illuminate the objective nature of the Bible. These are the questions of an understanding of the faith which has faced up to the matter itself and which asks its questions on the basis of the thing itself, which addresses them to an understanding of the faith that is still arrested at the beginning. . . . But dogmatic theology, too, must submit to the questioning of biblical theology. In biblical theology, it is faced with the Bible, which its own theological content serves to interpret. This can only strengthen the memory of dogmatic theology for the original meaning of its elements—the original meaning upon which it, too, depends in order to approach the essential matter."[9]

In this dialogue, systematic theology should not hope to gain everything from mere biblical vocabulary analyses. Initially, of course, such analyses seem strikingly novel and stimulating. But as long as these examinations of individual words contain no simultaneous questioning of the place they occupied in the *whole* structure of early Jewish or Hellenistic discourse and thought[10] (and this question is very often neglected today, too), the individual word analyses will be of little avail to theological thought. For instance, at the beginning of the nineteen fifties, a kind of liberation was experienced in the Church in German-speaking countries, when it became known that the New Testament μετανοειν did not simply mean "doing penance" but "conversion", and referred to a wholly personal turning of man to God. Nevertheless, the potentiality of this word in the New Testament, and certainly its deep significance for Christian theology, remained ineffective so long as, on the one hand, there was no consideration of the fact that, for the early Jewish mind, this word was indissolubly connected with the idea of the *Law* and the way, and, on the other hand, there it was not noticed that this word seldom occurs in the preaching of Jesus, when compared with the Jewish preaching of the time; and so long as it was forgotten that Jesus did *not* adopt any very emphatic line within the religious mentality of the time, whose special concern was the conversion (*tšwbh*) of man.

No less confusion would result from an attempt to use a simple biblical word analysis to decide which "concept of grace is really revealed by Scripture, and which is not." If the knowledge that the unity of Scripture does not mean a monotonous sameness (or the "sort that results when all the appropriate sayings are arrayed together...) and that the Bible is on the contrary full of the most

[9] H. Schlier, *op. cit.*, pp. 32–3.
[10] Cf. J. Barr, *The Semantics of Biblical Language* (Oxford, 1961).

difficult but at the same time potentially rich antitheses",[11] and yet is the *one* word of the *one* God (without that implying that "a simple harmonization of various scriptural assertions is permissible on the categorical level"),[12] so that the ever-new quest for the "centre of the Gospel" becomes pointless—if this recognition on the part of systematic theology brought about a new understanding of the development of dogma, together with the courage to sustain the contradictions of its "accounts and words" (K. H. Schelke) without any false harmonizing, no one would be happier than the exegete himself.

Nevertheless, neither in this kind of demonstration of the development of the Bible, nor in simply pointing out that individual dogmatic biblical sources are untenable, nor in the thematic treatment of individual major ideas, nor in biblical expositions in relation to theological questions of the moment, is the exegete really carrying out the specific service which he feels he is called to perform for the Church and its theology.

Convinced that the humanity in the person and work of Jesus of Nazareth was imparted to God's Gospel in the most open and therefore decisive way, but convinced too that this Gospel is mediated to us only through the witness of the first believers, who were children of *their own* time, and in no way impregnated with God's Spirit *in everything*, the exegete will primarily—and above all—concern himself with the knowledge of the person and work of Jesus himself,[13] as it is portrayed and as it is to be understood against the background of Jesus' own time. From this point on, he will consider the first development of the tradition of this Gospel, but also in terms of the threats to it—from the first witnesses up to the different New Testament writers. It will not disconcert him in the process to know that the necessary philological and historical assertions will bring the objection that his work is not up to date, and is therefore unproductive; for "exegesis must use all the means of philological science to examine a great number of words and terms only in the hope that it will come across an

[11] K. H. Schelke, "Heilige Scrift und Wort Gottes", *Wort und Schrift* (Düsseldorf, 1966), pp. 45–56, 50–1.

[12] W. Kasper, *Dogma unter dem Wort Gottes* (Mainz, 1965), p. 121.

[13] Cf. F. Mussner, "Der historische Jesus und der Christus des Glaubens", in *Exegese und Dogmatik* (see note 2 above), pp. 153–88; W. Trilling, *Fragen zur Geschichtlichkeit Jesu* (Düsseldorf, 1967).

important word".[14] Inasmuch as the exegete undertakes this work not only as a faithful member of the Church of his own time, but as a living human individual, he will certainly do it in the hope that decisive questions and helpful answers for both aspects will emerge.

In one aspect, he will make use of contemporary philosophical discourse; in the other, he will merely pose a question for further consideration, as, for example, when the difference between Jesus' call for unfailing confidence (Mk. 4. 3–8) and the first Christian inculpation of those in whom proclamation would seem to have borne no fruit (Mk. 4. 13–20)[15] causes him to ask whether a renunciation of such explanations of evil (which abandon the sinner in his guilt rather than help him to understand his unhealthy situation more profoundly) is not an essential part of the divine Gospel.

Another exegete, on historico-critical grounds, will feel himself duty-bound to avoid taking up a direct position on questions of the moment, on the basis of the biblical text, but without allowing anyone to interpret his reticence as a "refusal to help".[16] Even though it is understandable that systematic theology also expects the exegete to answer the question of the modern understanding of property, marital morals as they really are, the arrangements of institutional law, and so on, the following is nevertheless true: "Even the New Testament does not ordain any specifically Christian material indications . . . the New Testament writings do not of themselves establish a concrete universal ethos."[17] Therefore, if the exegete is unwilling to make any untenable and extreme assertions that would help no one in the end, he can *also* have to refuse to make a concrete statement, and only offer a pointer instead.

The dialogue between exegesis and systematic theology, which is necessary for both and required by the nature of the case, can certainly be furthered if each side is aware of the wishes *and* the possibilities of the other. The fruitfulness of this dialogue will, however, ultimately depend on the extent to which both exegete

[14] K. H. Schelke, *op. cit.*, p. 49.

[15] Cf. J. Jeremias, *Die Gleichnisse Jesu* (Göttingen, 1958), pp. 65–7, 130 f.

[16] Cf. A. Vögtle, "Fortschritt und Problematik der Neutestamentlichen Wissenschaft", in *Exegese und Dogmatik* (see note 2 above), pp. 53–68 (esp. 58–61).

[17] A. Auer, *op. cit.*, p. 77.

and theologian are on the one hand wholly desirous of making the Gospel of God (handed down in the community of the faithful and now recognized for what it is) comprehensible to the other, and on the other hand ready to confront one another with that trust without which there can be no genuine communication.

Translated by John Griffiths

Bruno Dreher

Exegesis and Proclamation

I. The Theology of Proclamation: A Basic Problem

JUST when the Church has put an epoch-making emphasis on the
Bible in divine service,[1] the basic rule of homiletics ("from
exegesis to preaching") is being fundamentally questioned, both
by Protestants[2] and by Catholics.[3] It is no longer a question of the
combination of exegesis and meditation, but of whether a theology
of proclamation can assist preaching in regard to the exegesis of
biblical texts, and meditation in a given situation.

The problem arises from the now considerable criticism of
historico-critical exegesis. Some ask whether it is not itself responsible for the lack of reference to reality and Church life, by reason
of its uncertainty whether biblical texts, as a theological inheritance, can be restated in any binding fashion for our own times;
and because of the question whether events in time (as a kind of
"second text") accord with the biblical texts, and the contention
that a socially-conscious theology radically affects the nature of
biblical texts.[4] Today, therefore, what has long been taken to be
an obvious presupposition of all ecclesiastical activity and discourse
—that preaching and ecclesiastical action have to "prove"

[1] *Ordo lectionum missae*, 25 May 1969.
[2] Erich Grässer, "Von der Exegese zur Predigt", *Wissenschaft und
Praxis in der Kirche und Gesellschaft*, 1971, vol. 60, pp. 27–39; E. Kittel,
"Muss die Bibel im Mittelpunkt des Religionsunterrichts stehen?", *Evan-
gelische Religionspädagogik* (Berlin, 1970), p. 341.
[3] *Gemeinde des Herrn. 83 deutscher Katholikentag. Tagungsbericht*
(Paderborn, 1970), pp. 432–3.
[4] E. Grässer, *op. cit.*, pp. 27–8.

themselves exegetically[5]—has been basically questioned. It is thought to be of wholly secondary importance that exegetical homiletics is still unusual in the Catholic Church,[6] that priests often have no appropriate grounding in their theological studies, and that there are no homiletic aids to help make the transition from the stage of pietistic biblical study to textual exegesis—in fact, something like these aids is only just beginning to appear for the new order for Sundays and holydays.[7]

Certainly, until now, there was a tendency to get entangled in the apparatus of exegesis or to succumb to the restrictions of the historical text; even though the enthusiastic high phase of exegesis in Catholic circles (from 1950 to 1965[8]) is now past, it is true that after the biblical encyclical of 1943 (*Div. aff. spir.*)—certainly the most significant document of Pius XII's pontificate—and the conciliar constitution *Dei verbum*, a return from scientific scriptural exegesis to the understanding of the Bible met with in the nineteen twenties and 'thirties (which was really a biblical pietism[9]) is no longer conceivable. It is increasingly evident that we are now in a scientifically-determined phase. Scientifically-oriented exegesis—so I believe—is part of the essential task of proclamation: "There is every opportunity for the Churches in the Bible—if they can make it a living voice in the contemporary consciousness."[10]

II. Historico-critical Exegesis an Essential Tool of Proclamation

The protest against the scholarly exegesis of the specialists is to some extent the result of a supposed (or actual?) inadequacy in the

[5] G. Otto, "Thesen zur Problematik der Predigt in der Gegenwart", in: P. Cornehl & H. E. Bahr, *Gottesdienst und Öffentlichkeit* (Hamburg, 1970), pp. 34 ff.

[6] Cf. *Initiativen* (Vienna, 1970), No. 4/3, pp. 13-4.

[7] Cf. Kahlefeld-Knoch, Schreiner, Läpple, Dreher (all since 1966–70), in *Dienst am Wort* (Freiburg).

[8] Franz Kamphaus, *Von der Exegese zur Predigt* (Mainz, 1968); Albert Höfer, *Predigt und heutige Exegese* (Freiburg, 1968); B. Dreher, *Die biblische Unterweisung im katholischen und evangelischen Religionsunterricht* (Freiburg, 1963).

[9] Celestien Charlier, *Der Christ und die Bibel* (Frankfurt a.M., 1969), pp. 23 ff.; N. Lohfink, *Bibelauslegung im Wandel* (Frankfurt a.M., 1967).

[10] K. Jaspers, *Die Atombombe und die Zukunft des Menschen* (Munich, 1968), p. 360.

approved method of exegesis: in, that is, critical historical research.[11] In reality—according to the biblical encyclical of 1943[12]—exegesis should be oriented to the basic concern of biblical hermeneutics: the elucidation of the meaning of the word of God (of the kerygma). The tasks of a homiletically polarized and historically critical exegesis and, negatively, the possible dangers for proclamation, may be summarized as follows:

Hermeneutics demands[13] a proficient textually critical and literary-critical elucidation of the text, and an up-to-date translation. Exegesis hampers preaching if the approach is really the kind of grammaticalism that is irrelevant or peripheral to the meaning. Rahner's remark[14] applies here: "Since the pulpit is the place where the directive, life-giving word of God, that affects our conscience and our heart and should change our life has to be proclaimed, and since a church is the place where God's truth (even though expressed in men's words)—and *not* human problems concerning God's word—is to be pronounced, it is not the place for learned discourses on disputed points or theological niceties." At another point in the same article, Rahner says, aptly: "It would be wrong to think that it is impossible to state the Christian faith before a congregation without explicit recourse to the question of this kind of theological problematics. According to circumstances, the preacher must be aware of such problems, and take note of them in the process of proclamation; he must interpret the biblical texts in regard to their content in terms of faith, but without going into ultimately irrelevant exegetical problems concerning the text. However, if he preaches responsibly and unpretentiously on the substantial faith of the Church, he will certainly express the faith of the Gospel and of the Church without any harm to his conscience as a scientifically aware theologian."[15]

Yet, according to the encyclical cited, the duty of establishing and preaching the kerygma with due regard to the literary kinds

---

[11] E. Grässer, *op. cit.*, p. 83.

[12] *Div. aff. spiritu*, 30 Sept. 1943, ASS, 35 (1943), pp. 297–236, in: *Enchiridion biblicum*, 265–232 (Naples & Rome, 1961).

[13] *Ibid.*, art. 546.

[14] K. Rahner, "Häresien in der Kirche heute?" in: *Theologische Akademie*, 5 (Frankfurt a.M., 1968), pp. 60–87.

[15] *Ibid.*

operative in the Old and New Testament writing, is strictly requisite: "... *antiquorum denique modus loquendi, narrandi scribendique innumeris exemplis illustratur. Haec omnia ... sacrarum Litterarum interpretes quodammodo invotant adque admonent, ut ad Divina Eloquia penitius perscrutanda, illustranda clarius, lucidiusque proponenda, tanta hac luce data alacriter utuntur.*"[16]

This means, on the one hand, that the preacher is not to indulge in intellectual dogmatizing without expressing the basic witness of the biblical situation historically, and without being acclimatized to Scripture; and, on the other hand, that he is not to spend his time on questions of literary genre, because it is of no use to the congregation to know that the Christmas stories in Luke are *haggada*, i.e. didactic stories. The exegete must beware above all of elaborating in an historically imaginative way, of evoking detail, of dramatizing, psychologizing, localizing and modernizing in a way foreign to the hagiographer—"This is no longer bearing witness in faith to the risen Lord, but at the best the provision of soporifics, a stimulus for family reminiscences or regression into a comforting, childish dream-world."[17] Of course the German bishops' statement also applies: "For example, the gospels cannot be grasped onesidedly as confessions of faith, but must also be evaluated as historically oriented documents, which in their own way offer us a true picture of Jesus and his activity. Therefore conscientious research cannot consider itself dispensed in advance —even in regard to the infancy narrative—from the quest for the historical background."[18] No more may a thorough exegetical exposition dispense with the quest for the traditional and editorial history of the text.[19]

Finally, the hermeneutical principle of context (life of the Church, dogma, liturgy and social behaviour) demands a responsible consideration of the actual effective history of the inspired word of God up to the present. Scientific exegesis is indispensable when it leads to a more profound grasp of God's word; but it has an inhibiting effect in biblical exegesis, and historically, if it

[16] Art. 546, *op. cit.*
[17] K. Frör, *Bibelhermeneutik* (Munich, 1961), p. 294.
[18] To licensed preachers: 22 Sept. 1967.
[19] *Ibid.*, No. 26.

deviates from and becomes an obstacle to the kerygma in regard to individual problematical details or scholarly questions of interest primarily to the specialist. Of course proclamation is possible henceforth only if there is contact with sound exegetical scholarship. The theological assertion must always stand up to historico-critical questioning. But the biblical witness to Christ, however, must be linked with the life of the Christian in the Church and in the world—backwards into the Old Testament and forwards into the present-day situation.[20] Similarly, Kurt Frör states: "Exegesis will do justice to the actual kerygmatic intention of these texts only if the links are duly established: both those which lead back to the expectant community of Israel (Lk. 2. 38), and those which lead forward to the coming fulfilment of the kingdom of God."[21]

One can only agree with Ernst Fuchs' apt comment: "The historico-critical method of interpreting New Testament texts has done its work when the word is made to inspire the preaching of the word."[22] The contention is untenable that the texts we have inherited awaken no response in modern man, and that this deficiency can be compensated by additional efforts to concern oneself with the questions of one's own time. There is an interaction between the search for up-to-date relevance and the theological content of the text; it is a feedback process. There is an incipient danger that the primary "whence" of theology will be taken as not the biblical text but the worldly *status quo*. The end result would be a theology that replaced the criterion of "listening to the word" with that of social relevance, grace with assent, and the Gospel with the Law, thus nullifying (while elevating) itself and the Church. "Theology for the times cannot be replaced by a theology of the spirit of the times. It was always and is now only obtainable by means of a conscientious exegetical concern for the biblical text."[23]

One has to agree with Bultmann's opinion, as it appears as the inspiration of the Catholic theologian Peerlinck's *Rudolf*

---

[20] F. J. Schierse, "Weinachtliche Christusverkündigung: Zum Verständnis der Kindheitsgeschichte", in *Bibel und Leben* (1960), pp. 217–22.

[21] K. Frör, *op. cit.*, p. 288.

[22] Cf. E. Grässer, *op. cit.*, p. 35, in *Die der Theologie durch die historisch kritische Methode auferlegte Bestimmung*, pp. 219 ff.

[23] *Ibid.*, pp. 35, 38 ff.

Bultmann als Prediger; Verkündigung als Vollzug seiner Theologie. Kerygma und Mythos als Problem der Predigt (Hamburg-Bergstedt, 1970): "We are united in seeing preaching as the proclamation of the word of God as it is borne witness to in the Bible, and that it must be understood as discourse that touches the heart, and that in this discourse Jesus Christ himself speaks to us. We are also one in seeing the task of preaching as the exposition of the Bible translated in such a way that it is understood by modern man; and therefore one in thinking that preaching must also be oriented to the particular situation of its recipients."

III. Scientific Exegesis in Preaching the Word

It was only to be expected that the vast amount of Evangelical Bible preaching would ensure that the critical question soon came to the fore. The basic thesis of H. D. Bastian's work[24] runs something like this: Proclamation cannot follow on a biblical, dogmatic, or liturgical *a priori,* nor can it depend on an *a priori* of ecclesiastical structure, but must derive from the question posed by the hearer. This last determines the hermeneutical search for meaning in, say, the biblical texts. Of course the problem of man considered historically ought not to be the sole source, or form the entire matter of preaching. One consequence of such a procedure would be the following: "The biblical call to love one's enemy remains private and irrelevant so long as it is not categorically translated into the language of the political world. Wars arise from hypermobile prejudices which are physically unleashed in force of arms. In this respect the propaganda about loving one's neighbour or one's enemy has never had any braking power. Something that can nullify explosive prejudices is to be sought only in the liberating power of the political question, which requires a political answer because it makes us aware of the real consequences of our actions. . . ."[25]

From this viewpoint, it is a question not of a kerygmatic summons but of a political question! Otto states clearly:[26] "The Church is the forum for consideration of religious life themes and

[24] *Theologie der Frage* (Munich, 1969).
[25] H. D. Bastian, *op. cit.,* p. 179.
[26] Cornehl-Bahr, *op. cit.,* pp. 34 ff.

inquiry into the relevance of Christian tradition for contemporary life. The consequences are the critical reception, interpretation ... and alteration of traditional contents. The introverted, unworldly monologue and indoctrination, which are inimical to dialogue, are based on a verbalized form of reflection without any action. If preaching does not emerge from the narrow form of a sermon enclosed within divine service, and does not take various forms (adult discussions, dialogue sermons, radio, journalism, talk), it cannot tackle the actual and really urgent questions of those to whom it is addressed."

Questioning and provocation can succeed with a congregation only if the art of rhetoric is cultivated—above all on public occasions. The biblical proclamation obtained a new local value in the context of public problems: the assumption (virtually a law) that preaching is the direct imitation of the exegesis of a passage in the Bible must be seen as historically-conditioned in theological terms; it can no longer be presented without any real consideration of its truth value. The history of proclamation shows that the road "from exegesis to preaching" is anything but sacrosanct. In the last thirty years it has contributed to the impoverishment of theology—however understandable the impulse may be historically.

In place of the above-mentioned law, we also have the novel question of the function of biblical tradition in Christian discourse. What is the role of biblical texts in preaching? Nowadays preaching is no longer accountable to biblical texts, but to theology. Measurement by the yardstick of the biblical text restricts the horizon; and the relevance of the ancient text for contemporary audiences is often decided positively in advance, despite intensive hermeneutical activity. But the real sort of theological responsibility means that Christian discourse must show itself to be "a word" in the actual responsibilities of those to whom it is spoken; it must induce a confrontation with tradition; then biblical tradition will become relevant for today's world. But it is not *a priori* the sole ground, not the automatic starting-point, not an unquestioned authority, and not the obvious goal of Christian discourse. Not only preaching on a text but preaching on a theme is absolutely necessary today. More precisely, theology must be a

combination of systematic, socio-ethical and practical theology.[27]
These are theses to which one may indeed assent, though with
some care. They indicate a move from exegeticism to an insistence
on the problem theme.[28] Nevertheless, it must be affirmed that the
original biblical witness pure and simple is the *norma normans*
of the word of the Church. It must be remarked that Catholic
preaching was always closely linked with the effective history of
the biblical word, that is, with the statement of tradition in an
historically actual sense, and is therefore not faced with the annoy-
ing problem that confronts Protestants, who have to consider
how a two-thousand-year-old message can be translated into a
modern industrial age. A constant dogmatic and living reformula-
tion makes the word of the Bible effective in the present-day
world (Vatican II).[28a]

IV. Exegesis and Proclamation Today

Jörg Zink's translation of selected texts from the Bible is a good
example of something that makes one sit up.[29] The linguistic aliena-
tion-effect his style has is in no small measure produced by suitable
pictures of contemporary life facing the translated passages. The
precise, exegetically accurate text is freed from any kind of
biblicism and becomes a joyful reality for modern men.[30] Horst
Bannach's work[31] almost deserves the title of a basic model for this
kind of book. For a number of passages, an additional text illus-
trating some modern problem is supplied, together with a photo-
graph evoking a particular situation: the result is a striking
portrayal of a contemporary meaning for something said long
ago.[32] The scientifically established text forms the background,

[27] Cornehl Bahr, *op. cit.*, pp. 39–41.

[28] G. Otto, *Denken um zu glauben* (Hamburg, 1970).

[28a] R. Marlé, *Das theologische Problem der Hermeneutik* (Mainz, 1965),
p. 123.

[29] Stuttgart, 1967.

[30] The fact that a few of the translations and adaptations were not too
happy does not affect the book itself.

[31] *Wunder beweisen gar nichts—Problem des 20 Jahrhunderts im Spiegel
der Apostelgeschichte* (Stuttgart, 1971), p. 32.

[32] E.g., Acts 8. 9–24: the Holy Spirit doesn't provide the goods: he en-
lightens men and sees to it that they go to work; one fish suffices only for

but the interest is supplied wholly by the present; the introduction of modern problems enables any preoccupation by exegetical considerations to be avoided.

A classic model for the preaching situation is to be found in the *Predigtstudien* series.[33] In clear contradistinction to the well-known multi-volume modern Evangelical sermon guidebooks, which all try to apply exegesis,[34] what the two authors have done here is to pair every biblical thought with a socio-homiletic passage. A good piece of preaching keeps to the basic rule that human concepts and questions, problems and worries compose the dominant hermeneutic principle in explaining the Bible. The new-style biblical sermon-book by G. Otto, *Denken um zu glauben*, uses sample sermons to illustrate its basic homiletic principle: that although biblical tradition is the relevant object of preaching, it is neither its sole reason nor the automatic starting-point for all statements, nor the obvious goal, nor the unquestioned authority to be expressed in the actual theme.[35] Without going into the quality of individual examples in the book, one can only agree that faith has to do with the objective reality of human existence, and indeed can only be intended thus. This work carries out a decisively humane existentialization of the texts.

Jean Cardonnel,[36] R. H. Fuller[37] and P. Pokorny[38] also make original contributions to the problem of actualizing the message. Pokorny's work is oriented to a typically existential type of modern preaching: the political sermon.[39] Today exegesis, precisely in its scientifically established form, can only be the starting-point and norm of Christian discourse, which it is absolutely necessary to affirm if exegesis is confronted with a non-biblical (dogmatics)

---

one day, whereas learning how to fish will provide food for ever. Acts 10. 9–20: pure-impure can be applied to the colour question today.

[33] Ed. E. Langer, P. Krusche, D. Rössler (Stuttgart & Berlin, from 1967).

[34] E.g., G. Eichholz, *Herr tu auf meine Lippen* (Wuppertal, various editions 1939–62); *Calwer Predigthilfen* (Stuttgart, 1962–66)—OT and NT vols.; W. Stählin, *Predigthilfen*, 4 vols. (Kassel, 1961–6); L. Schmidt (ed.), *Die Schriftauslegung*, 5 vols. (from 1967); *Kasualien*, 16 vols., ed. W. Brandes; *Göttinger Predigtmeditationen* (journal: Göttingen, from 1945).

[35] See Cornehl-Bahr, *op. cit. supra.*, pp. 34–43.

[36] *Brasilianische Predigten* (Munich, 1970).

[37] *Wunder Jesu in Exegese und Verkündigung* (Patmos, 1967).

[38] *Der Kern der Bergpredigt* (Hamburg, 1969).

[39] M. Müssle, Ed., *Der politische Jesus—Seine Bergpredigt* (Munich, 1969); D. Sölle, *Politische Nachtgebet in Köln* (Stuttgart & Mainz, 1969).

or a non-theological text (human anthropology). The attentive preacher will find plenty of such texts (problematical themes) available: in the present theologico-ideological and anthropological debate, in the information media—press, television, radio—in literature and modern poetry—to mention only the most obvious sources. To cite a few examples of the kind of comparison I mean, one might refer to Lk. 10. 35–7 (the Good Samaritan) in conjunction with a picture of the helicopters bringing aid to East Pakistan. The German, American and British helicopter pilots are Samaritans for the starving survivors of the catastrophe. Jn. 20. 24–31 (the Thomas passage) can make its point when Solzhenitsyn's *Cancer Ward*[40] is used to show how under the attrition of the cancer ward and the bureaucratic dictatorship, a man can only remain human by deriving an inward peace from something inhuman (humour). The preacher might well adopt Georg Lukács' judgment:[41] that, above all in the attempted resolution of the final phase, the book discards humour as the most certain expression of the unconquerable nature of man, and gets caught in a kind of querulous plebianism in the Stalinist manner. This provides the preacher with the occasion for a sermon on Christian (paschal) humour.

The preacher is not only entitled but bound to avoid any literary aestheticism and to speak directly to a world in which the essential problem of the work in question is grounded. Phil. 4. 4–9 (rejoicing in the Lord) can be really strikingly conveyed by the evocation of young people's questioning of the world represented by our society to be found in Wolfgang Bauer's *Magic Afternoon*.[42] The boredom portrayed there is a spiritual problem and, of course, an eminently religious one too. What is really at question underneath everything is God in worldly language. The only possible answer to the God-vacuum is "helpless brutality". We may take the play as an attempt to articulate boredom on the stage, and to show forth in the rhythm of actions the nature of inactivity—looking at oneself in the glass, smoking, dancing, drinking, putting records on the gramophone. Suddenly everything explodes. Pointless hatred erupts. Birgit, wholly incensed,

[40] English translation: London, 1968–69.
[41] *Alexander Solzhenitsyn* (London, 1971).
[42] Berlin-Neuwied, 1968.

stabs Joe. In this situation, the message of the biblical passage supplies a meaning and a goal, and offers a hope of joy in the future if the future is loving.

1 Cor. 15. 56 can be set against Paul Celan's famous poem *Schwarze Milch am Morgen*, which portrays the vile reality of death in a concentration camp where Jews were murdered; if the poem is used to counteract an excessive and illusive conception of Easter, then the precise exegetical interpretation becomes a genuine interpretation for men in our time.[43]

The basic formula is as follows: Scientific exegesis is the correlative of a homily oriented to the present.

[43] *Folge mir nach*, stage 5 (Zürich, 1969).

Translated by John Griffiths

Oswald Loretz

The Church and Biblical Exegesis

AT present the Catholic Church is passing through a phase of great unrest and uncertainty. Many bishops, priests and laymen would attribute this state of affairs—to some extent at least—to the work and results of modern biblical exegesis. Whatever the part played in such arguments by conjecture, the undemonstrable, and fears and desires, which are then resolved into the unanalysable whole of an almost mythical idea of the magically destructive power of scientific exegesis, one should not overlook the core of truth in these ideas and feelings. An attempt to grasp the present relation between the Church and scientific exegesis brings one face to face with a situation which, historically, psychologically and theologically, is extremely complex.[1]

The present circumstances can and must be seen as the result of a process of historical development. The still dominant and regrettable obliviousness within the Church to the importance of history is often treated lightly in the matter of wrong ecclesiastical attitudes and decisions; but we must not forget that, from Galileo and Foscarini[2] to Vatican II, the official Church has regarded modern biblical exegesis with considerable scepticism, and has even rejected it. There is a reluctance to admit all the

[1] For a presentation of the situation from a more exegetico-dogmatic viewpoint, see, e.g., R. E. Murphy, "The Role of the Bible in Roman Catholic Theology", *Interpretation*, 25, 1971, pp. 79-89.

[2] A.-M. Dubarle, "Les principes exégétiques et théologiques de Galilée concernant la science de la nature", *Revue des sciences philosophiques et théologiques*, 50, 1966, 67-87.

blunders, mistaken decisions and suppression which the official Church and accepted theology have been guilty of in regard to exegesis from the time of Galileo to Vatican II. If one examines the individual stages of the confrontation between Church and exegesis from Galileo on, only astonishment seems a fitting reaction to the impatience, enmity to science and brutal suppression[3] of free scientific work in the service of the Church. However, since the concerns of modern biblical science were, until Vatican II, of profound and consuming interest to only the small number of exegetes proper, and both the teaching authority of the Church and dogmatic theologians succeeded in keeping this group and its exemplary effects in quarantine within the Church, and in isolating it almost completely, it was possible for a long time to devalue the problems of exegesis as the errors of turbulent minds led astray by the modern spirit. However, this had to change as soon as the findings and approaches of scientific biblical exegesis won more acceptance within the Church. This development—already heralded by the Modernists at the start of the century—came to a premature close with the end of World War II. At the same time the modern scientific approach had already become so entrenched that, on the one hand, a persecution and suppression of individual scholars was no longer viable and, on the other, any attempt to put down the modern views on Scripture now widespread among clergy and laity was impossible in practice. Therefore the magisterium had to change its tactics and review the traditional position. The predominant and widely-held opinion—hammered in above all by the biblical encyclicals—was that the Church had always encouraged exegesis anyway, and that there was an unequivocal though upward line of development marked by the papal encyclicals on the Bible. This interpretation, too, easily overlooks the facts which point in another direction. In a just perspective, all that this view represents is an attempt (after the moment of

---

[3] See, e.g., in respect to the affair of the *Manuel biblique* (1923) the correspondence between M. Blondel and J. Wehrlé (*Bulletin de littérature ecclésiastique*, 71, 1970); also M. Delcor, "Une correspondance inédite de l'époque moderniste. A propos de la question biblique en France," *Bulletin de littérature ecclésiastique*, 70, 1969, 214–9.

"conversion") to see past practice as the necessary and logical preliminary phase of present circumstances.[4]

Within Catholic theology, one question is often thought to be of pressing importance: that is, whether the official Church has to approve of whatever may be the current position in scientific research, or whether biblical scholars are duty-bound to try to get their work recognized by the Church. This, in the light of my previous remarks, is a pseudo-problem. For recognition or rejection of scientific exegesis depends—as history shows—on the extent to which modern thinking has sunk in generally, and on the possibility or impossibility of administrative interventions in the process of scholarship and research. The question of the power that ecclesiastical authority has over biblical scholarship has to be seen in connection with the general question of how far the Church has any right to take up a position in regard to scientific problems, methods and findings. At present all we can say is that the opinion dominant in the past that the Church was entitled to give judgment on everything—in whatever form— that had anything to do with the interpretation of Scripture, is now groundless, and that a different question is now pertinent. It might be put something like this: when it became quite impossible to exercise an ecclesiastical hegemony over biblical interpretation that would mean opposing modern science,[5] another problem arose: Has the Church any right to give an absolute judgment on biblical exegesis itself? Clearly, circumstances have so developed as to make No the answer here too. Despite exceedingly great efforts to the contrary, Church leaders have been unable to prevent the incursion of modern scientific thought into Catholic exegesis.

The original reason for the crisis in exegesis has now proved to be a focus of crisis for the whole Church; exegetical unrest now forms only a part of the general situation in the Church: ". . . which is constituted by the many unanswered questions that have accumulated through the centuries, the immense

[4] For the psychology of conversion and the associated apparatus of legitimation, see P. Berger and T. Luckmann, *The Social Construction of Reality* (New York, 1968).

[5] In traditional interpretations, an *a priori* result was proposed to and demanded of science. Cf., e.g., the debate on the biblical account of creation, the question of evolution, and so on.

development of human knowledge in all directions, and an all-encroaching secularization . . .".[6]

The relationship between biblical science and the Church is marked by a deep psychological animosity. Whereas the so-called official Church from the time of Galileo maintained in regard to the efforts of biblical scholarship that it, the authority, enjoyed the right to the last word in exegetical questions, and insisted on this right in particular instances, time showed this claim to power to be just empty words; in the sense, that is, that despite the justness of the underlying dogmatic point, its sole practical significance was to allow ideological justification for a tight control of biblical science. From the beginning, it was clear that in the long run a general theological principle cannot be transformed into a metaphysical principle for support of the *ancien régime*, but can be no more than the expression of a reality within the Church, which never exists as a "pure culture" but only in a particular historical form. In the meantime it has also become questionable as far as *theology* is concerned whether it is possible to identify the Church with its teaching authority, or the judgment of the Church (in practice) with Roman declarations.[7]

Even with Foscarini and Galileo it was clear that traditional theology and the official Church were psychologically unable to tackle the new questions proficiently, precisely because these problems opened traditional attitudes and modes of thought on fundamental issues to discussion, and replaced them with new forms. I shall refer to some of the connected problems in the remarks that follow.

If we see the start of the new exegesis, or of the modern exegetical problem, as coincidental with the rise of the natural sciences, then even the case of Galileo appears as an attempt by the Inquisition to define the interpretation of Scripture as the exclusive field of operation of "theology" and of the official magisterium.[8] The layman had no right and no access to biblical exegesis; it was reserved to a circle which, from this point on,

---

[6] K. E. Skydsgaard, *Orientierung*, 35/4, 28.1.1971, p. 39.

[7] H. Kümneringer's article on this point has been found very useful: "Sache der Kirche, 'judicare de vero sensu et interpretatione scripturarum sanctarum'" (deals with the understanding of this proposition at Trent and Vatican I), *Theologische Quartalschrift*, 149, 1969, pp. 282-96.

[8] Cf. note 7 above.

increasingly and obviously got out of touch with progress in the sciences. In this system, biblical interpretation was first of all clericalized and then finally appeared as a concern of the magisterium of the Church. In Catholic circles this development led to an exaggerated attitude that could no longer find any justification in the Bible, but (necessarily) believed it was justified by the results of the Reformation. The subjectivism stemming from the Reformation had to be given a counterweight in the form of an objective institutional court of judgment.

This view of the "infallible" doctrinal, hierarchical and clerical administration of truth within the Church, together with a theological teaching system ensured by the charism of infallibility, is itself still widespread among historians as the "Catholic perspective". Hence, for example, Aubert (in his article "Church History as an Indispensable Key to Interpreting the Decisions of the Magisterium", *Concilium*, 7, 6, 1970; American edn., vol. 66) writes: "The theologian's task stems from the word of God, but . . . in the Catholic perspective, is presented and applied to new situations by the Church's magisterium. One of the theologian's basic pieces of equipment, therefore, is as exact a knowledge as possible of what the magisterium has said on any particular point and the degree of authority attaching to this statement. Is a particular definition by the magisterium covered by the charism of infallibility which it enjoys in certain well-defined cases—very rare ones at that? And, if it is, what exactly has it said, what is the real point of the definition covered by the guarantee of infallibility and so to be taken as irreformable?"

In the "Catholic perspective", then, the identification of Holy Writ and the Pope-and-Bishops becomes possible. The parallelization of inspired Scripture/Magisterium/Episcopate then leads, for example, to the following argument: "Just as God at one time dispensed his word through the medium of human writers and their world of ideas, so today he speaks to us through such intermediaries, preserving his word, showing its applicability, and extending it to more extensive problems. It is not more difficult to believe that he performs this action of preservation, assertion and interpretation through the pope and the bishops in union with him (Vatican II, *Lumen Gentium*, a. 18 and 22), than to believe that he at one time ordained the composition of the Bible by those holy writers. The two are so closely connected that whoever denies the magisterial apostolate of the Church will end up by denying the divine nature of Holy Writ." (A. Kolping, "Geschichtliches und dogmatisches Denken sind keine Gegensätze", in *Anzeiger für die katholische Gesistlichkeit*, Supp. 8, Sept. 1970.)

However, the new exegesis brought further basic assumptions of traditional theology—above all the value of tradition—under attack. Whereas until then a problem could be settled in the scholastic sense by the assembly and examination of traditional assertions, the new viewpoint introduced angles which were wholly novel. The new psychological burden seemed especially painful since it not only denied the value of traditional knowledge, but encouraged an attitude which took the current state of knowledge as its starting-point, and allowed tradition validity only in so far as it agreed with the exegete's own findings. This intellectual approach was deemed irreconcilable with the fundamental thinking of Christian tradition. The main reason for rejecting the new demands would really seem to have been that the new scholarship recommended an anti-traditional approach. Henceforth the yardstick for all questions was not to be the statements of the venerable dead who were traditionally held to be holy men, but the results of experimental, non-clerical science. Since this realm of science was beyond the competence of the Church, it was thought that the assertion and radical application of the traditional claim to power was the only way to preserve the Christian inheritance. The question whether it was at all possible, on the basis of Scripture and the belief of the Church, to justify such a claim to authority, was suppressed by reference to the right of the *status quo*.

The new approach, with its constant readiness to revise traditional views, necessarily caused greatest distress among those who, in the footsteps of patristic-scholastic theology, had long ago converted a development of ecclesiastical teaching and its dependence on particular chronologically-conditioned viewpoints into a system of eternal, unchangeable truths. The new attitude, which recommended conviction based on experiment and facts, could be interpreted from the old viewpoint only as relativism, novelty-seeking and contempt for tradition. The helplessness of the old position in regard to the new feeling for science and life produced a ready irritation in the conservatives; this they could express only in confident rejection of, and refusal to recognize, facts, and in a dogmatic-metaphysical contempt for the new ideas. In this respect, the ground of reliable, quiet theological reflection or of the requisite charitable form of discussion within the Church had long been abandoned for factional feuding and heresy hunting. In essence, the trial of Galileo and the previous judgment on Foscarini determined the various forms the struggle took right up to Vatican II.

The questions of the relation between the biblical and the natural-scientific world views, as it remained alive up to Vatican II, may now be seen as resolved. The obvious victory of the new way of thinking and the implicit acknowledgment of guilt in regard to the errors of the past, which Vatican II managed to produce, should not, however, make us blind to the fact that the battle-lines merely shifted and that the old struggle continues in different forms. We are now confronted with the fact that the traditional attack on biblical science has ceased since Vatican II, and has been replaced by a disregard of exegesis. This change of fronts deserves closer consideration.

The new questions which deeply concern people in the Church and in the developed nations (the problem, say, of human procreation and of personal freedom, or of the relation of faith to a technologized form of life dominated by science) are only slowly and laboriously taken into account by the Church. The old positions are no longer defended by recourse to a traditional interpretation of the appropriate passages in Scripture, but by ignoring every serious scientific confrontation with the pronouncements of the Bible. Since theology and the magisterium know full well that the Bible offers no grounds for the defence of traditional ecclesiastical-theological viewpoints (as defended, for example, in *Humanae Vitae* or the encyclical on celibacy), the official ploy is to avoid any confrontation with exegesis. Vatican II, therefore, announced a wholly new phase in the relationship between biblical science and the Church. The Bible now disappears as a factual basis for arguments contrary to the expectations awakened by Vatican II, and is replaced by an appeal to nature and the "history of the

Church". In this process the Old and New Testaments are not counted as Church history.

The degree to which study of the actualities of the Bible and the position of the hierarchical establishment can part company in the treatment of ecclesiastical questions of the moment, is to some extent obvious from the following discussion: "*Liselotte Görres*: Where does the bishop get the right to demand the charism of celibacy from a man who feels he has a vocation to the priesthood, even though it is a non-biblical requirement? *Cardinal Höffner*: The bishop derives this right from the self-understanding of the Church. The Church, as the Council says, believes that the Lord will give us sufficient vocations to the priesthood which coincide with the vocation to the celibate life. That is the self-understanding of the Church at present. The bishop is a member of the college of the world episcopate and acts as such. No one—and I also stated this in my ten points—has a right (a so to speak subjective right) to be a married priest. The Church has laid down additional principles of selection for admission to ordination, for instance a school-leaving certificate or the need for pastors. The imposition of rules of selection is not unjustified" (from *Über den Zölibat der Priester,* ed. L. Waltermann (Cologne, 1950), p. 52 (the record of a West German radio broadcast)).

According to Cardinal Höffner's argument, the traditional form of biblical evidence is replaced with the philosophical concept of "self-understanding", and the Church is clearly no more than the hierarchy of the Church. However, the fact that uniform action by the world episcopate in a question which does not concern the belief of the Church cannot be asserted to be the "self-understanding of the Church" is quite forgotten. The careless treatment here of the notion of the Church is clear, too, in the statement that "the Church" has laid down other principles of selection—of the order of a school certificate.

This state of things is, however, to be judged extremely positive—in one respect. It is the result of a development from the time of Galileo to the present, which has now come to an at least theoretically premature conclusion. For the unilateral preference for the metaphysical, "church-historical" mode of argument only implicitly raises the question whether the Church may ground its claims and teaching solely in metaphysically "church-historical" terms, and whether it is permissible for it to separate the history of God and men, as described in the biblical accounts, from the so-called "history of the Church". From an historical and psychological as well as cultural and historical viewpoint, despite many asseverations to the contrary, we have now reached a full stop in the relationship between exegesis and the Church. The high theoretical rating of Scripture by the last Council is opposed to an official treatment of scientific biblical interpretation which in thought and practice deviates not fundamentally but only inescapably (that is, by virtue of changed sociological conditions) from the attitude of the Inquisition of earlier times and of the Biblical Commission.

The tension between biblical science and the Church includes weighty theological as well as historical and psychological problems. Of primary interest in this regard is what the concept of the "Church" means in any particular instance, when the relationship between the Church and biblical scholarship is in question. Undoubtedly a large number of the participants in the discussion who come from hierarchical or theological circles identify the Church straightforwardly with the magisterium. This mode of thought developed after Trent and dominated the field until the present day. In this sense, the Church is set over against biblical exegesis. It must be recognized that this interpretation of the notion of the Church has no foundation in Scripture or in ecclesiastical tradition. The Church was certainly never simplistically identified with the magisterium. This exaggeration of the concept of the Church gave rise to the sort of opposition in which the Bible appears here, and the sole correct and ultimate interpretation by the magisterium there. This theory and attitude prevented important aspects from receiving proper consideration. The impression was awakened that the magisterium could and must judge everything, and that when it gave a decision, the question was settled. Yet it remained quite clear that the Church could not explain the scientific problems of modern biblical science in the old authoritarian way, and that the Bible was not a book to be subjected to permanently valid explanations on the part of the magisterium. As a book for instruction in faith and proper conduct, the Bible has always been far more than a collection of documents for official ecclesiastical decisions. In this respect, too, Vatican II ought to have made its pronouncements about Scripture much clearer.

The modern biblical debate since Galileo and the dispute between exegesis and the magisterium can be understood only when it is seen how, by its acceptance of new methods, biblical scholarship put in question the *conventional* claim to truth of Holy Writ and hence that of the magisterium. At the end of the nineteenth and the beginning of the twentieth century, this point often appeared openly in the contention about the *question biblique*. If, in the sense of the new form of exegesis, the Bible is a book containing errors and chronologically conditioned viewpoints which are still comprehensible for us only in an historical perspective, then the recognition of this necessarily implied a withdrawal of the theology which, after Trent, increasingly put a halo of eternal and unalterable truth about the statements of the magisterium. For those biblical scholars schooled in philology and history, this claim to absolute truth on the part of the Church and the pronouncements of the magisterium was merely a remnant of times past. Since, however, the magisterium and dogmatic theology believed that even the slightest trace of an error in Scripture would lead to the assumption that the magisterium could go wrong, and that in this case the very bases of traditional theology and official ecclesiastical practice would be affected, the struggle over this question was especially bitter. Only Vatican II was able to reach the decisive turning-point in this regard. It discarded the patristic and medieval ideology of an absolutely infallible Bible and began to speak of biblical truth.

This acknowledgment leads what is virtually a separate existence within theology and Church life, and again we are faced with the danger that both the magisterium and theology will either continue to ignore the word of biblical truth, or once more interpret it in a metaphysical-systematic sense. On the one hand, statements of the magisterium (e.g., *Humanae Vitae*) are surrounded with an official aura of infallibility and absolute truth, and in theology the actual or possible errors of the magisterium are discussed with dogged seriousness—*rabies theologica* (see, for example, the theological and ideological discussion by

Küng and Rahner in *Stimmen der Zeit*, 187, 1971, pp. 43–64; 105–6; 145–60).

From the viewpoint of the Bible, however, neither the errors of Scripture nor those of the magisterium are decisive, but the power of truth made evident. From the standpoint of the biblical concept of truth, for instance, it is of no account how many errors there are (or are not) in *Humanae Vitae*. Ultimately, what comes under debate is only whether this document presents, e.g., an articulation of Christian truth which is directive for the life of the contemporary believer, or merely an all-too-human piece of theologizing on behalf of an out-of-date way of thought which contradicts the biblical condemnation of the divinization of nature. If theology believes that its primary task is to establish exactly how far the individual documents of the magisterium are binding, then it will remain sunk in a kind of thinking that takes the truth of the Bible not so much as an indication of how life should be lived and an exhortation about behaviour, but as a suitable field for the exercise of theory. From the biblical viewpoint, the prophet's words, "How can you say, 'We are wise and the law of the Lord is with us'? But behold, the false pen of the scribes has made it into a lie" (Jer. 8. 8) apply, today as well, to the hierarchs and theologians who seek to lay down the truth. There would be a lot of strong words if the prophetic understanding was again accepted that the false pen of the scribes can be found in the hands of exegetes, theologians, bishops and popes alike. Not errors but lies are the serious danger: refusal of duty, flinching from novel situations, and the interpretation of God's truth in favour of human intentions, desires and ends, and for the securing and increase of human power.

*   *   *

The understanding of the nature of the Spirit obtaining up to the present was surely of supreme importance for the relation between biblical science and the Church. The Spirit of God, which brought Scripture into being, was—from Trent onwards —seen increasingly as the unique possession of the magisterium and as the guarantee of its infallible teaching authority. Yet the history of the Bible and of the early Church shows that no human bounds are set to the Spirit of God in the Church. The Spirit speaks through men, whom he chooses freely. Therefore Scripture is interpreted amiss when its inspiration is used to conclude that only the magisterium possesses the Spirit, and hence administrative power over biblical truth.

*   *   *

In conclusion, it should be remarked that the present tension between biblical scholarship and the Church is very much determined by Church history and its problems as well as by questions peculiar to the modern era. Therefore it would be unjust to complain only of the one aspect: i.e., the hierarchical establishment and the theology of incomprehension, suspicion and resentment. Regrettable, too, is the present verbal exaggeration of the capabilities of exegesis as a result of the essentially acceptable pronouncements of Vatican II on Scripture, on the one hand; and the dominant disregard in practice of Scripture by the hierarchy in the treatment of existing problems of Church life and conditions in relation to modern culture. This state of affairs must continue until there is a change in circumstances within the Church. The relations between exegesis and the Church will be difficult so long as it remains impossible under modern conditions to satisfy the old requirements of Scripture. In this regard, it is not essentially a question of the defence of traditional truths but of accommodation to modern civilization. So long as the ecclesiastical hierarchy is able to see the various branches of the Church only in the perspective of past orders, so long as it offers out-of-date views of human procreation as binding, or classifies the clergy as if it were a medieval caste, the Church will continue to assert what is different and contrary to Scripture. In this case, it is true both of biblical science and of the hierarchy and the magisterium that the Bible is an uncomfortable book, which admonishes us for our truths, our dogmatism, injustice and lack of love, and at the same time helps us in our human weakness. Anyone who carefully follows the strained relations between Church and exegesis from the time of Galileo will be unable to offer an easy or simplistically reductive judgment on the errors and omissions on the part of the Church. In this respect, above all the discrepancy between the statements of Vatican

LIBRARY
KENRICK SEMINARY
7800 KENRICK ROAD
ST. LOUIS, MISSOURI 63119

II on exegesis and their lack of application in ecclesial theology in the post-conciliar period require consideration. Not a small part of the guilt for this latest development must be placed on the shoulders of the exegetes themselves, who are to a large extent weary of offering—with prophetic courage--biblically based viewpoints on questions of moment. Even though this is humanly understandable, it is not justified in biblical terms. The biblical scholars have withdrawn behind the wall of "science" and have stilled their tongues. They devote themselves to science, and play with the biblical texts as if they had nothing to say on all that is now under discussion and debate in the Church. Once the Church-and-exegesis problem in the traditional sense has disappeared, the danger arises that exegesis, because of its attachment to an outdated conception of science, will not perceive, and will lose, its own particular function in the Church today.[9]

[9] C. J. Peter (*Interpretation* 25, 1971, pp. 93-4) offers an admirable account of the new malaise which threatens biblical scholarship.

Translated by John Griffiths

Bas van Iersel

Theology and Detailed Exegesis

I. An Exegete and a Theologian discuss Mark 1. 1–15

THE geological specimens the American astronauts brought back from the moon have been sent all over the world to very many different centres, where teams of scholars will study one fragment with the greatest care and attention. This procedure is based on the assumption that the results of detailed research into a single stone may be decisive for man's theory about the origin of the moon, and even that of the Milky Way. The principle, then, is that an understanding of the microcosm is important for our understanding of the macrocosm. Is the exegete's detailed study of a short Bible text of similar importance to the work of the systematic theologian?

It is, of course, obvious that no general theological theory can be formed on the basis of one passage or a few short passages of Scripture. Any theological theory ought to be based on the whole of the Bible, of which the "history of the effects" of Scripture forms an integral part. Several factors have to be borne in mind here. Firstly, the exegete knows that no total view is possible without a knowledge of the most important parts of Scripture, and that this overall idea and detailed exegesis are complementary, and dependent on each other. In the second place, the biblical scholar is bound to take short passages as his point of departure, although a total view of the Bible may always be at the back of his mind. The systematic theologian, too, can only come to general theoretical conclusions by a study of details. The question then arises as to whether exegesis of a short text can be used for this purpose, and to what extent and in what way such exegesis is able to further the speculations of the systematic theologian.

To put this question concretely, I have summarized a previously published analysis of Mark 1. 1–15,[1] a passage chosen for its special functional importance at the beginning of one of the gospels.

1: The beginning of the gospel of Jesus Christ (the Son of God).

2: As it is written in Isaiah the prophet: "Behold, I send my messenger before thy face, who shall prepare thy way;

3: the voice of one crying in the wilderness: prepare the way of the Lord, make his paths straight—"

4: *John the baptizer appeared* in the wilderness, preaching a *baptism of repentance for the forgiveness of sins. 5: And there went out to him all the country of Judea, and all the people of Jerusalem; and they were baptized by him in the river Jordan, confessing their sins.* 6: Now John was clothed with camel's hair, and a leather girdle around his waist, and ate locusts and wild honey. 7: *And he* preached, *saying, "After me comes he who is mightier than I, the thong of whose sandals I am not worthy to stoop down and untie. 8: I have baptized you with water; but he will baptize you with the Holy Spirit." 9: In those days Jesus came from Nazareth of Galilee and was baptized by John in the Jordan. 10: And when he came up out of the water, immediately he saw the heavens opened and the Spirit descending upon him like a dove; 11: and a voice came from heaven, "Thou art my beloved Son; with thee I am well pleased." 12: The Spirit immediately drove him out into the wilderness. 13: And he was in the wilderness forty days, tempted by Satan; and he was with the wild beasts; and the angels ministered to him.*

14: Now after John was arrested, *Jesus came into Galilee,* preaching the gospel of God, 15: and *saying, "The time is fulfilled, and* the *kingdom of God is at hand; repent,* and believe in the gospel."

II. TRADITION AND EDITING IN MARK 1. 1–15

The first fifteen verses of Mark's gospel are best analysed today —although the method is not without its opponents—in accordance with the principles of form criticism and an examination of

[1] See *Vox Theologica*, 39 (1969), pp. 169–179.

the editing of the text. This method presupposes that the authors of the gospels used small, existing units of tradition, and that Mark's gospel was written before the others, with the result that the later gospels cannot be quoted to explain the Marcan text. In other words, the editorial elements in Mark can only be eluci-dated, on the one hand, by isolating the previously existing literary units and, on the other, by identifying the linguistic and stylistic peculiarities of Mark as these appear in the whole of the gospel.

III. Verses 1. 1 and 1. 14–15

There is every reason for regarding Mark 1. 1–15 as a literary unity. This unity is recognizable from the so-called inclusion established by the use of the word *euaggelion* (gospel, good news) at the beginning and at the end of the passage. This is one of the key-words in Mark's gospel, and we may therefore assume that v. 1 is the evangelist's own heading, an assumption that is strengthened as soon as we try to see vv. 1–8 as a previously exist-ing traditional unit. This, however, entails difficulties. The first is that this kind of quotation usually occurs not in traditional units, but rather in passages into which they have been inserted by the evangelist concerned. The second is that so little is said about the *euaggelion* of Jesus Christ in vv. 1–8, that v. 1 cannot really be linked with the passage about the Baptist (vv. 1–8). Because of these difficulties, it is therefore better to regard v. 1 as an editorial be-ginning on the part of Mark himself.

The close of the passage, vv. 14–15, requires rather more careful thought. On the one hand, these verses join what follows to what has gone before, thus functioning as a kind of hinge. On the other hand, they also conclude the account of the Baptist and the one baptized. The presence of Mark himself can be recognized in the occurrence—twice—of the word *euaggelion*, once of Mark's favourite word "proclaim" or "preach" (*kērussein*) and of the phrase "after John was arrested".[2] This does not mean that Mark

---

[2] See W. Marxsen, *Der Evangelist Markus* (Göttingen, ²1959), pp. 22–25. Marxsen also believes that the mention of Galilee is editorial (p. 36), which is in accordance with his view of the whole gospel. There are, of course, certain objections to this.

may not have used a datum of tradition: "And Jesus came into Galilee, saying, 'The time is fulfilled, and the kingdom of God is at hand; repent'". But it does seem very unlikely that these words were linked in tradition with the preceding passage or that they formed a single whole with the previously existing passage about the calling of the first disciples (vv. 16–20). Because the section has a rather general character, striking us as a *résumé*, it is possible that it was written by Mark himself. In any case, the end of v. 14 ("preaching the gospel of God") and the end of v. 15 ("and believe in the gospel") must be attributed to Mark himself.

IV. Tradition and Editing in vv. 2–8

Three parts of this section are probably the result of editing. The first is the group of quotations and the evangelist's introduction (vv. 2–3), which are related to the so-called "reflection quotations" in which a certain connection with the Old Testament is established afterwards. This affinity is confirmed by Matthew's simplification of this quotation, his use of it elsewhere and his adaptation of the introduction to his introduction to the other quotations (see Matt. 3. 3).

Quotations of this kind are never traditional. They are always the result of editing. This is confirmed by the fact that v. 4 would, from the literary point of view, be the beginning of an account if it were prefaced by "and"—"And John the baptizer appeared. . .". The "and" would automatically be dropped when the passage was included in the gospel.

Verse 4 probably also contains another editorial addition, "in the wilderness, preaching". Several arguments can be put forward to show why these words did not form part of the account of John's appearance. In the first place, the words "in the wilderness" refer to two places—the activity of the Baptist is described in v. 5 as taking place "in the Jordan" and, as far as baptizing is concerned, this is obviously a much more suitable place. To give two places in this way is certainly not customary.

The second objection, which many commentators have pointed out, is that baptizing in the desert is hardly usual. Even if the words "in the wilderness" are attributed to the evangelist, there is a further discrepancy which has so far received little attention.

The text reads: "preaching a baptism of repentance. . .". Nowhere else in the New Testament do we find "baptism" as the object of the verb "preach". This is not at all surprising, because the object of "preaching" is not "baptism," but Christ or the gospel. If we approach this datum from another point of view and try to find the verb which belongs to "baptism", we discover that it is, apart from this particular passage and the texts dependent on it (Luke 3. 3; Acts 10. 37; 13. 24), always the same—it is "baptize" (Mark 10. 38, 39; Luke 7. 29; 12. 50; Acts 19. 3–4). Finally, if we recall that "preach" (*kērussein*) is one of Mark's favourite words, there can be no doubt that the beginning of the account about John was originally: "And it happened that John baptized a baptism of repentance . . ." and that Mark himself inserted the words "in the wilderness, preaching".

Thirdly, as so many commentators have insisted, v. 6 is an addition.[3] This verse breaks the sequence in two ways. Firstly, a personal description of John, which one would in any case expect to find at the beginning of the account,[4] interrupts its dynamic flow. Secondly, those who are addressed twice as "you" in v. 8 are, from the literary point of view, left entirely hanging in the air if v. 6 is included. This is not the case if we read from v. 5 to v. 7.

Therefore Mark probably had this account at his disposal: "And it happened that John baptized a baptism of repentance for the forgiveness of sins. And there went out to him all the country of Judea, and all the people of Jerusalem; and they were baptized by him in the river Jordan, confessing their sins. And he said, 'After me comes he who is mightier than I, the thong of whose sandals I am not worthy to stoop down and untie. I have baptized you with water; but he will baptize you with the Holy Spirit'."

[3] See K. L. Schmidt, *Der Rahmen der Geschichte Jesu* (Berlin, 1919), p. 225; R. Bultmann, *Die Geschichte der synoptischen Tradition* (Göttingen, ⁴1958), p. 261; W. Marxsen, *Markus, op. cit.*, p. 20; L. Vaganay, *Le problème synoptique* (Paris, 1954), pp. 356–358.

[4] This is why this personal description is in a different place in Matthew, where it occurs after the summary of John's preaching in v. 2, and together with the quotation from Isaiah in v. 3. In Matthew, then, the description of the Baptist is placed in vv. 3–4 between the data concerning his proclamation on the one hand, and the mention of his activity baptizing in the river Jordan, on the other hand.

As far as its structure is concerned, this account is one of those short pieces or apophthegms, consisting of a brief outline of the situation followed by a statement. It is possible that it originated in discussions between the followers of Jesus and those of John. Its function would then be to show, by a statement made by the Baptist himself, that Jesus is greater than he. Be this as it may, the account certainly had a Christian source—this is clear from the language used[5]—and it deals with a comparison between the significance of John and that of Jesus.

Mark, then, included this account in his gospel after having adapted it. What is the real purpose of this adaptation? In the existing tradition, John was represented, not as a preacher, but as the one who baptized, and his words, as quoted by the evangelist, refer to baptism. But, in his process of adaptation, Mark adds two things to this image of John. In the first place, he calls John a preacher in the desert by adding different, but connected, insertions to the account. To v. 4, he adds "in the wilderness, preaching" (*en tē erēmō kērusson*), which corresponds to the second half of the scriptural quotation, in which John is described as a "voice crying in the wilderness" (Isa. 40. 3). Even more important is the second correspondence with the Old Testament. A little later in Isaiah (Isa. 40. 9), we find two references to the messenger of joy (*euaggelizemenos*) who calls out to Jerusalem and to the cities of Judah: "Behold your God, behold the Lord God comes with might".

Now the key-word in Mark 1. 2–8 is *euaggelion*. We cannot, then, escape from the fact that the author regarded John as the messenger of joy of Isa. 40. 9 and—what is even more significant—that he described the one whom John is announcing, Jesus, as "mightier" than John (Mark 1. 7), indeed as the one for whom the way had to be prepared (Mark 1. 3).

The second half of v. 6 also fits into this image. Going back to other traditional data about the Baptist (Matt. 11. 7–14; Luke 7.

[5] The fact that this is Christian language is indicated by the combination of "preach", "baptism", "repentance" and "forgiveness of sins" (cf. Luke 24. 47; Acts 2. 38), especially by the use of the expression "forgiveness of sins" (cf. Matt. 26. 28; Acts 5. 31; 10. 43; 13. 38; 26. 18; Col. 1. 14) and the expression "confessing sins" (cf. James 5. 16; 1 John 1. 9).

24–28[6]), we find that Mark also depicts John as a desert figure. At the same time, however, he also identifies John with Elijah by giving him, in the first half of v. 6, the garments in which the prophet was said to be dressed in 2 Kings 1. 8. This is also connected with the quotation from the Old Testament inserted at the beginning of Mark's account, a quotation (v. 2) which is derived from Mal. 3. 1,[7] which refers to a messenger sent to "prepare the way". This messenger is later, in Mal. 4. 5, identified with Elijah: "Behold, I will send you Elijah the prophet before the great and terrible day of Yahweh comes". What is more, Mark is not simply anxious to identify the Baptist with the prophet Elijah here. He is also pointing out that the time which is to follow John's appearance will be the "great and terrible day of Yahweh".

V. Baptism and Temptation (vv. 9–13)

Mark has apparently made no editorial insertions into the account of Jesus' baptism and temptation (vv. 9–13), but two important questions arise in connection with this section. The first is, did Mark join two traditions together here or did he simply use one single tradition? The second is, is there any indication of a long history in the case of these traditions (or this tradition)?

Many scholars think that the beginning of v. 9 is Mark's own editorial formula, but there seems little doubt in my opinion that this is an almost classical opening phrase. What is far less clear is where the already existing tradition ends in the passage under consideration. Does it include only the story of Jesus' baptism (vv. 9–11), with the result that the report of Jesus' temptation in the desert (vv. 12–13) has to be regarded as the remnant of a separate tradition, or do vv. 9–13 form one single tradition?

We must be careful, of course, not to be influenced here by the situation presented in Matthew and Luke, yet it is remarkable that both make a distinction between Jesus' baptism and his temptation: Matthew by inserting the word "then" (*tote*) (4. 1), and

---

[6] In Matthew and Luke, too, John is described as a desert figure, dressed in clothing which is contrasted with the soft garments worn at court, and as a prophet.

[7] Mal. 3. 1 is also applied to John in Matt. 11. 10 and Luke 7. 27. In Matt. 11. 14, the Baptist is also identified as Elijah.

Luke by inserting a genealogy (3. 23–38). Both also relate the temptation in a longer and more self-contained account. Both of these factors give their accounts of the baptism of Jesus a high degree of autonomy.

This is not so in the case of Mark. In the light of various textual data, it is probable that Jesus' baptism and temptation formed one single, previously existing traditional unit. For example, unlike the rest of the gospel, "the Spirit" (*to pneuma*) is used in vv. 10 and 12 without any further qualification.[8] It should also be noticed that the different parts of vv. 9–13 are similarly linked together ("and then", *kai euthus*, in vv. 10 and 12). Finally, the same cosmic language is used throughout the whole section. After Jesus' baptism by John, only heavenly and demonic powers are mentioned. The structure of the passage is therefore quite different from that of the Matthaean and Lucan accounts of the baptism of Jesus. Bultmann was perhaps nearest to the truth when he called it a legend of faith expressing what Jesus signified to the community which believed in him.[9] It is, however, not at all clear how this functioned in the community. It might have been used for instruction in Christian baptism, but no clear indication of this can be found anywhere in the New Testament.

F. Hahn has attempted to provide an answer to the question about the history of this tradition.[10] He is of the opinion that the story came about in two phases, and bases his view on Jewish-Christian and Hellenistic Christian characteristics in the account. The opening of the heavens, the appearance of the Spirit, and the voice from heaven, point clearly in the direction of a Palestinian tradition. In this Palestinian Christian version, however, the words "my Son" would not have appeared. The word used would have been "my servant" (*pais*)—it was only during the Hellenistic Christian phase that the word "son" (*huios*) would have been given a place in the story.

These two different levels can be recognized most clearly in the

---

[8] The "spirit" in Mark 9. 20 refers to the "dumb spirit" in 9. 17, and the absolute "spirit" has—within the antithesis spirit-flesh—an entirely different function.

[9] R. Bultmann, *Geschichte der synoptischen Tradition, op. cit.*, pp. 263–264.

[10] F. Hahn, *Christologische Hoheitstitel im Neuen Testament* (Göttingen, 1963), pp. 340–346.

different ways of speaking about the Spirit. In v. 12, the Spirit is the passing power which drives Jesus into the desert. In vv. 10–11, on the other hand, the Spirit is referred to as a permanent gift, making Jesus the Son of God. Hahn believes that v. 12 reflects Palestinian Jewish ideas, whereas the second reference, vv. 10–11, reflects the Hellenistic viewpoint.

Although this interpretation cannot be ruled out completely, I find Hahn's arguments unconvincing, mainly because the view that the word "servant" may have been used initially in 1. 11 rather than "son"—a view which is by no means new—is quite hypothetical. What is more, it is not at all clear in 1. 10 that, in that verse, the Spirit is bestowed on Jesus as a permanent gift, giving him permanent power to carry out his mission.

VI. The Beginning of the Good News (Mark 1. 1–15)

The great importance of this passage as a whole should now be clear. Very gradually, the author introduces Jesus as the Son of God. Because he says first that John was the prophet Elijah returning to proclaim the good news, there can be no doubt about the identity of the one who is to follow him, the one who is then presented to the reader, by the "voice from heaven", as the Son of God.

The author therefore reveals to the reader at the beginning of the book what is concealed from those who appear in the book until Jesus' death. In the light of Rom. 1. 3–4, Paul's good news (*euaggelion*) and Acts 13. 33, we may even ask whether the attentive reader is not reminded of Jesus' resurrection as well at the beginning of the book.

Is it, however, exclusively "good news" (gospel)? The book is offered as the "beginning of the good news" and I think we should take this seriously. The author tells us about Jesus, but not with the extreme clarity of the real *euaggelion*. This complete clarity only emerges at the end of Mark's book. Jesus is proclaimed in Mark 1. 1–15, on the other hand, in rather veiled Old Testament terms, as the *Kyrios*, then in the rather clearer language of the Baptist (vv. 4, 7), and subsequently in the even clearer presentation of Jesus as a word from heaven. Finally, Mark himself proclaims Jesus, letting all that has been said be heard again.

What is striking at the end of this passage is that Mark says very clearly that Jesus proclaimed the gospel (1. 14–15). He also makes it clear that the gospel proclaims Jesus as the one who died and has risen again. The good news is heard fully when this is said (see 1 Cor. 15. 1 ff.)—in other words, at the end of Mark's gospel (Mk. 16. 6). It is very tempting to think that everything that precedes this statement of Jesus' death and resurrection is part of the beginning of the good news. In other words, we may think of everything that Jesus did and said and everything that happened to him, including his own proclamation, as the beginning of the proclamation of the good news to the Christian community and to those outside it. This is perhaps why Mark used the aorist of the verb "to begin" (*ērksanto* or *ērksato*), followed by the infinitive much more emphatically and much more frequently than did Matthew and Luke.[11]

[11] See Mark 1. 45; 2. 23; 4. 1; 5. 17, 20; 6. 2, 7, 34, 55; 8. 11, 31, 32; 10. 28, 32, 41, 47; 11. 15; 12. 1; 13. 5; 14. 19, 33, 65, 69, 71; 15. 8, 18—twenty-six times in all; only nine times in Matt., six of these together with Mark—12. 1; 16. 21, 22; 26. 22, 37, 74. Matt. uses it once from Q—11. 7, and alone twice—4. 17; 11. 20. In Luke, this construction occurs nineteen times, but only three of these together with Mark—19. 45; 20. 9; 22. 23; only once together with Matt.—7. 24, and alone in 4. 21; 5. 21; 7. 15, 38, 49; 9. 12; 11. 29, 53; 12. 1; 14. 18, 30; 15. 14, 24; 19. 37; 23. 2.

Translated by David Smith

Piet Schoonenberg

Notes of a Systematic Theologian

I. Scripture and Tradition

THE way in which the systematic theologian reads Scripture deserves all the attention that is given to this question in this number of *Concilium*. As a Catholic theologian, I believe that Scripture should be read together with post-biblical tradition or —as van Iersel would say—together with the "history of the effects" of Scripture. I also think that this could be a common meeting ground between ourselves and our Protestant colleagues.

According to modern exegesis, the Old and New Testaments are the literary result of a very dynamic history of interpretation, and I am particularly alert to the continuation of this history after the closing of scriptural revelation. Christology underwent a positive, yet critical, process of development from biblical times to Nicaea and Chalcedon. I am convinced that the basic christological definition of Chalcedon was a culminating point in post-biblical christology, but is not a fruitful point of departure for reflection today,[1] with the result that we now have to turn back from Chalcedon to Scripture. We must therefore try to answer this question: Can every interpretation of Scripture provide the point of departure for further theological reflection?

[1] W. Pannenberg, *Grundzüge der Christologie* (Gütersloh, 1964), p. 300 ff.; P. Schoonenberg, *Hij is een God van mensen* ('s-Hertogenbosch, 1969), pp. 49–181 (*The Christ*, New York, 1971, pp. 50–175).

II. Exegesis and Systematic Theology

Although openness of mind, leading to an existential under-standing of Scripture, is a gift of the Holy Spirit, we are still obliged to attempt to understand the Bible by means of the human and scientific method of exegesis, and the systematic, scientific theologian is in turn bound to make use of this exegesis. This means, as Carl Peter argues in this number, a co-operation between the exegete and the systematic theologian, who always synthesizes on the basis of the existential problems of the contemporary world. He is therefore in constant need not only of the building materials, but of the criticism provided by the exegete, who can above all teach him that he will always gain more insights and perspectives from Scripture than from any contemporary syste-matic theology. Another valuable lesson that the systematic theo-logian can perhaps learn from the exegete is that Jesus and the study of the New Testament are not identical with a criticism of society! Finally, he may also learn from the Scripture scholar that the authority on which he bases his study is less exclusively proleptic than Pannenberg, for example, would have us believe.[2]

On the other hand, the systematic theologian can also ask the exegete a number of critical questions. The first is this: Is the exegete himself perhaps not too much a systematic theologian? This is also a question exegetes ask each other, using different words. Oscar Cullmann has established numerous links, for in-stance, between *mar* and *kyrios* and between the "Son of Man" and Paul's "last Adam". He has also drawn attention to the possibility of Jesus' expressing his mission by applying christo-logical titles to himself, or having them applied to himself.[3] Cull-mann has been criticized by Hahn and Reginald Fuller, whose christological studies are much more strictly based on form criticism (or rather on what I would call the sifting of form and sources).[4] They therefore make a sharp distinction between Jesus' understanding of himself and the three levels of interpreta-tion in the New Testament (the interpretations of the Palestinian

[2] W. Pannenberg, *op. cit.*, pp. 47–61.
[3] O. Cullmann, *Die Christologie des Neuen Testaments* (Tübingen, ²1958).
[4] F. Hahn, *Christologische Hoh eitstitel* (Göttingen, 1966); R. H. Fuller, *The Foundations of New Testament Christology* (London, 1965).

Jewish community, of the Hellenistic Jewish community and of the Hellenistic mission to the Gentiles). We may therefore reasonably ask whether these scriptural scholars are not really disguised systematic theologians—perhaps not systematic theologians "of the titles" like Cullmann, but systematic theologians "of the levels".[5] The same question is also asked by van Iersel in his article—he is of the opinion that Hahn's distinction between two levels in the interpretation of Jesus' baptism, based on the antithesis between "servant" and "son", and between the Spirit that comes now and that remains permanently with us, cannot be proved.

I should like to ask all exegetes of the school of Bultmann—and that means almost all exegetes—whether they do not often lock themselves up inside their literary analysis. After all, in examining a definite passage, should the exegete not speak as far as he can about the facts themselves? This may sound rather naïve, but I am aware that we can reach Jesus only through the interpretation of the Christian community, and I am in full agreement with what Marxsen has said about this.[6] It is, however, also possible to discover Jesus within this interpretation of the community, so long as the criteria for this are critically examined. As a systematic theologian, I am indebted to Fuller for having done this, and I would have liked van Iersel to have done the same—but perhaps I am asking too much of exegesis of one pericope. Once, at a congress at which exegetes said many excellent things about the literary form and theological background of Jesus' baptism and transfiguration, I was disappointed because they said so little about Jesus himself. Surely our theology, preaching and faith would gain immensely if this were done?

III. Summaries and Detailed Exegesis

The exegetical works that the systematic theologian should study first are, I believe, summaries, and firstly those dealing with

[5] Dietrich Ritschl has accused Fuller of an "overly systematic categorization" in *Memory and Hope* (New York and London, 1967), p. 24.
[6] W. Marxsen, *Anfangsprobleme der Christologie* (Gütersloh, [5]1967), p. 11.

a definite theme. I have learnt a great deal about original sin from Dubarle and Scharbert,[7] and about christology from Cullmann, Hahn and Fuller. But exegetical studies of Paul, John and of the whole of the Old and New Testaments are of importance to the systematic theologian, because he can learn from them precisely how important a part a given theological theme plays in Paul, John or the whole Bible. Very pertinent comments about this are made by Joseph Zalotay in this number, and Lyonnet has pointed out the connection between Paul's doctrine of original sin in Rom. 5. 12–21 and his whole christology.[8]

Going further, we may say that the systematic theologian who has studied the christology of the New Testament is also bound to be aware of the "initial problems of christology" (to use Marxsen's term), and of the fact there is almost no christology in Q and the letter of James. I am not claiming that it is wrong that there should have been a change of emphasis since New Testament times—on the contrary, it is good that more attention has been given to God's universal salvific will—but I do insist that the systematic theologian should take seriously the critical question with which Scripture confronts him: namely, does he not tend to underestimate some themes and overestimate others?

So much, then, for summaries. The theologian must, however, be on his guard against constructing a system or summarizing data on the basis of detailed exegetical studies. As far as the structure of the universe is concerned, he can best make use of the results achieved from detailed research into a single stone brought back from the moon. This will prevent his theory from being too abstract. What I learn from van Iersel's study of Mark 1. 1–15 is something about the growth in the New Testament of christology and of the interpretation of the Baptist, both of which are of value to contemporary theology.

---

[7] A.-M. Dubarle, *Le Péché originel dans l'Ecriture* (Paris, 1958); J. Scharbert, *Prologomena eines Alttestamentlers zur Erbsündenlehre* (Freiburg, 1968). I am also indebted to Lyonnet's detailed studies.

[8] S. Lyonnet, "La problématique du péché originel dans le Nouveau Testament", in E. Castelli, ed., *Le mythe de la peine* (Paris, 1967), pp. 101–108.

IV. The Interpretation of Jesus

Mark knows the *euaggelion* of Jesus Christ, just as Paul knows the *euaggelion* of God concerning his Son (Rom. 1. 1–5). Mark's confession of Jesus as the Son of God begins only after Jesus' death (Mark 15. 39); in proclamatory formulations which Paul takes over (Rom. 1. 1–5) or which are attributed to him (Acts 13. 33), this sonship is brought about, or at least manifested, in Jesus' resurrection. The full *euaggelion* of Jesus as the Son of God therefore takes place only after Easter. Mark makes this clear throughout the whole of his book by surrounding Jesus' manifestations as the Messiah and the Son of God with the double wall of Jesus' commandment to silence (the "messianic secret") and the disciples' lack of understanding. It is only after the Son of Man's resurrection that the vision of him can be made public (Mark 9.9). In connection with the full proclamation after Easter, Jesus' own proclamation is only the "beginning of the *euaggelion*" (Mark 1. 1); these words could therefore be the title either of the pericope 1. 1–15 or of the whole gospel of Mark.

Jesus' sonship of God is made fully manifest after his resurrection. According to the ancient christology of Acts (2. 32–36), Jesus was made Lord and Messiah by his resurrection and exaltation and, according to an even earlier level in Acts (3. 20 ff.), he will be the Messiah when he returns. This interpretation of Jesus' relationship with God—and consequently of his saving significance for us—therefore begins with his resurrection and *parousia* and moves back to his life on earth and to the beginning of that life. The New Testament thus begins with a christology of the exaltation and goes back to an incarnational christology. We have evidence in Mark 1. 9–13, then, that Jesus' divine sonship was first established after his resurrection, and that it was concluded from this that he was the Son of God from his baptism onwards. In other words, before raising Jesus as his Son to his right hand, God addressed him as Son and gave him full power at his baptism.

What I have done in the preceding paragraph is to situate the detailed exegesis of Mark 1. 1–15 within the whole of the New Testament. I should now like to add a few notes as a systematic theologian. *Firstly*, the movement forwards has the logic of faith in the Easter event. I agree with Pannenberg that any justification and confirmation of that faith that are seen in Jesus' resurrection and exaltation must also apply to the whole of Jesus' person and life, including the beginning.[9] *Secondly*, it is probable that Jesus' baptism was an historical point of departure for his consciousness of his own mission. Jesus' baptism must have been an historical fact, because, in view of the difficulties that Jesus' disciples had with John's, the opposite might have been expected in the Christian tradition (see Matt. 3. 14). But the significance of Jesus' baptism with regard to his appearance and his person may also have been based on an historical experience. We have Jesus' word that the kingdom of God begins with John (Luke 16. 16 par) and the statement in which he links his power to that of John (Mark 11. 28-20 ff.). Because they equate Jesus and John, both indicate a strong possibility of historicity, and may therefore describe an experience of Jesus, namely that, since John and his baptism, his power had been awakened in him and God's Spirit had come over him.[10] If this is so, then both Mark and Luke contain a recollection of Jesus' experience—he sees the heavens open and the Spirit descending on him and he is addressed. *Thirdly*, Mark ceases with the baptism of Jesus—there is no reception of the Holy Spirit (Luke 1. 35; Matt. 1. 18), and no incarnation of the Word (John 1. 14). Although a christology proclaiming Jesus' sonship of God is possible in Mark without any incarnation or clear pre-existence, the Son of God is still placed at the centre of the cosmos. At the end of Mark 1. 1–15, he is placed between God and Satan and between the angels and the beasts and, according to the added conclusion (16. 9–21), he has to be preached to the whole of creation (16. 15).

A christology which makes Jesus come from God as the Son of God or Logos, and situates him in God's eternity, is not necessarily wrong, but it is limited. Christology illustrates the saving significance of the Jesus who lived, died and rose again, but, in throwing light on any other, pre-existent meaning of Jesus, it must not detract from his complete humanity. If it is used as a point of departure, rather than as an illustration, then all that can be used to show Christ's true humanity is the model of Chalcedon (the "two natures"), with all its insoluble difficulties

[9] Pannenberg, *op. cit.*, pp. 61–69.
[10] Fuller, *op. cit.*, p. 116 ff.

and its danger of reducing the hypostasis of Christ's human nature.

V. The Interpretation of the Baptist

The interpretation of John the Baptist grows alongside that of Jesus. I have already mentioned the texts in which the Baptist is equated with Jesus and in which a power "from heaven" is behind the appearance of both (Mark 11. 28–30 par). The kingdom of God too begins with John (Luke 16. 16; Matt. 11. 12; see also Matt. 3. 2). A recognition of the part played by Jesus in the coming of the kingdom of God—a part of which he was himself conscious (Luke 11. 20; Matt. 12. 28)—led, in the light of the resurrection, to an interpretation of Jesus as the definitive turning-point and therefore of John as his precursor. This development is clear in the gospels—in the synoptics, the Baptist has his own message, in John he is only the witness to the light and the Bridegroom's friend and everything that he says points to Jesus.

In Luke 1 and 2, we have an account of the proclamation and the birth of the Baptist derived from his disciples; there is no reference to Jesus, and it is merely confronted externally with the story of the proclamation and the birth of Jesus.

In Mark 1. 1–15, we can see the growth of the interpretation of the Baptist by means of van Iersel's distinction between the sources. In the source used by Mark, the Baptist is already the precursor—he baptizes with water, Christ with the Holy Spirit (Mark 1. 8 par; Acts 1. 5). In Mark, the Baptist plays the part of Elijah and of the messenger of joy (Isa. 40. 3), both of whom appear in the desert; he is also identified with the messenger in Mal. 3. 1. This may be derived from a tradition of the Baptist, in which he is seen as the immediate precursor of God himself, as in the accounts in Luke 1 and 2. But, in Mark's editing, the Baptist's role as the precursor is seen in the light of God's coming *in Jesus*, the Son of God. The unusual "proclaiming as a herald" (*kērussein*) in Mark 1. 4 points in this direction.

This gives the systematic theologian much food for thought. As we have seen, an earlier interpretation of Jesus can expose the lack of balance of a later interpretation, which has caused many aspects of these earlier layers of tradition to become "lost truths".

For example, the truth that has been forgotten in the christocen-
tric interpretation of the Baptist is that Jesus took over the
Baptist's message and, in an even more general sense, that he
was the heir and the continuation of Judaism.

The exegetes of the *New Quest of the Historical Jesus* are not
wrong to claim that only those words of Jesus which contrast both
with the community after Jesus' time (especially the Palestinian
Jewish community), and with the Judaism of Jesus' own time,
can be historically proved to be Jesus' own words. We should,
however, limit Jesus' influence and personality unjustifiably were
we to reduce these simply to his very few contrasting statements.
Jesus was, after all, a personality who continued to live in his
community, and was at the same time the heir of the tradition
in which he lived. It is precisely in this that he was original. It
was, I think, Wellhausen who said that Jesus was original in
what he did *not* say, and he is to some extent right. Pannenberg
is more completely right, however, in saying that Jesus gave
priority *in* Judaism to the eschatological expectation of the future
rather than to the law.[11] In this way, Jesus' originality is not to
be found in adding to the Jewish tradition, but in causing a revolution within it and taking it beyond its frontiers. It is therefore
important to find out what Jesus may have learnt from those who
handed down that tradition (we no longer accept Thomas
Aquinas's view that the Son of God did not learn from men),[12] and
what the apocalyptic writings and the Baptist meant to Jesus.
Catholic theologians have long been alert to God's preparatory
work in Mary, and now they are invited to give similar attention
to his work in John the Baptist.

[11] W. Pannenberg, "The Revelation of God in Jesus of Nazareth", in
J. M. Robinson and J. B. Cobb, eds., *Theology as History* (New Frontiers
in Theology III) (New York, 1967), pp. 101–133, esp. p. 103 ff.

[12] *Summa theol*. III, q. 12, a. 3, after Thomas had, contrary to his earlier
opinion, accepted a real increase of acquired knowledge in art. 2.

Translated by David Smith

Joseph Zalotay

Original Sin

THERE is no lack of accurate presentations of the doctrine of
original sin as held by St Paul.[1] Every major commentary on
Romans has to discuss this point, every New Testament theology
has to touch upon it. Dogmatic theologies approach the subject in
their own way. They may present the doctrine and support it with
arguments (old method) or they[2] may present the exegetical consensus with dogmatic commentary as a first step towards Augustine, Trent and our times.

The present paper intends to contribute to the dialogue between
exegete and dogmatic theologian.[3] Exegetes have already confronted Freud on original sin,[4] historians[5] have challenged the
theologian, and exegetes[6] have left their mark on modern dogmatic discussion.

The literal sense, the sources and their influence, the context
and its role in Rom. 5 have been almost definitively determined.
The theological sense of the passage has been narrowed down

---

[1] Abundant bibliography in P. Grelot, *Péché originel et rédemption dans
l'épître aux Romains: NRTh* 90 (1968), pp. 337–362, 449–478, 598–621; J. L.
Connor, *Original Sin: Contemporary Approaches: ThSt* 29 (1968), pp. 215–
240 .

[2] See P. Schoonenberg, in *Mysterium Salutis* 2, pp. 899–906, esp. 902 f.

[3] See H. Vorgrimler, Ed., *Exegese und Dogmatik* (Mainz, 1962).

[4] Grelot, *loc. cit.* (esp. the first and third articles).

[5] E.g. J. Gross, *Enstehungsgeschichte des Erbsündendogmas* (Basle, 1960–
1963); H. Haag, *Biblische Schöpfungslehre und kirchliche Erbsündenlehre*
(Stuttgart,[3] 1967).

[6] See note 2, and Haag, *loc. cit.*

infallibly by Trent. But dogmatic theology and exegesis together have not yet reflected sufficiently or with sufficient clarity and agreement on the limits inherent in the New Testament texts themselves.

These limits are twofold: some are specific to this problem and others inherent in the whole of biblical theology. To the first belong: St Paul's own tangential interest in the question, the first-century horizon of his theology, the idiosyncrasies of his Old Testament categories, the christology that necessitates Rom. 5, the possible scope of Rom. 5 in the light of Rom. 8 and especially of Rom. 9–11, and finally the limits of the "slot" generally set by Paul's christology and anthropology, into which original sin, personal sins, Satan and the "Powers" all have to be fitted by Paul himself.

Beyond Pauline theology, one has to take into account the absence of the problem in Johannine theology; the non-existence, in fact the material (non-logical) impossibility of an original sin in Jesus' doctrine; the late, artificial appearance of an Adam theology and of "solidarity"; the abundance of metaphors for the redemptive work of Christ, each of which requires an alternate conceptualization of sin and original sin; and finally, the extent to which Paul's views on the inspiration of the Old Testament determine his subjective evaluation of his own arguments.

I. The Inner Limits of the Theologies of the New Testament

Modern biblical theology, as a basis upon which the dogmatic theologian can reconsider the traditional position, has its limits set by the theological qualities of the New Testament itself. I submit that even a probing discussion of the truth content of New Testament doctrines[7] is clearly within the province not only of biblical theology but even of exegesis.

In this task of analysing and evaluating the various New

[7] This task includes the clear admission of the legendary character of some narratives, elementary demythologization of scenes like the Ascension, and the investigation of the relative merits of, for example, Pauline *versus* Johannine christology.

Testament theologies,[8] a certain coherence within the subject-matter is a natural guiding principle that must not be sacrificed to the analogy of faith. On the other hand, each particular doctrinal position has only a limited area for growth and influence.[9]

In view of the above it would be illegitimate to deny that in some vague form Paul did think of an original defect in Mankind-Adam[10] but it would be far more mistaken to enlarge the slot available for the negative solidarity in Adam. Paul clearly strains his vocabulary to insist upon the disproportion between the solidarity in salvation through Jesus and the sin that began with Adam.

Theological options also set unmovable barriers. I will list here a few of doctrinal character and a few others that determine theological conceptualization.

In the matter of sin: Monotheism necessarily requires a "Satan" as soon as sufficient reflection on evil has taken place. Sin in man then is traced to Satan. Example, direct influence, deception and divine permission are offered in the Old Testament as possible explanations of how Satan causes man to sin. In a religion insisting on the ethical, as the Old Testament does, individual responsibility requires discussion. Historical thinking and a naïve need for etiology will have to point out a first instance of human sin and of Satan's work. The sins of an epoch will be defined according to the needs of a later theological moment.

Etiology and philosophically naïve theories of imaginary collective personalities determine the thought on sin in similar ways. The promise can only reach Israel if they are physical descendants of Abraham. The Law is by Moses. Wisdom comes from Solomon alone, mankind from Adam and Eve. We need only mention collective responsibility as a basic tenet of the earlier theologies of the Old Testament, the long list of those who induced Israel to sin or caused the innocent to suffer punishment together with the guilty, the firm conviction that whole "evil" nations have to

---

[8] Some may be highly complex, such as Paul's; some merely inchoate, as the christology of Q.

[9] None of the soteriological phrases of St Paul satisfied him beyond the immediate needs of the context. Logos does not exhaust the mystery of Christ for St John.

[10] See J. De Fraine, *Adam et son Lignage, sine loco* 1959, p. 130.

be destroyed by immediate divine action, and the oscillation between the views that require a Messiah or only God himself to achieve this.

The monotheistic option ultimately bars theologies that tend to be negative concerning human nature. The core of personality must be the work of a good God. The discovery of individual responsibility similarly excludes a fundamental inability to observe some basic law. The formulation of God's relation to Israel as that of a Covenant[11] requires the inherent possibility of its fulfilment. God is just and rewards or punishes justly. Not even dualistic language could penetrate the core of Israelite theology.

Humbly, and with unique theological genius, the Old Testament stopped well before the line of the mystery of evil. This gives it its dignity as valid theology: not "gnosis" but truth. Man is free. Man was created by God. The serpent deceives. He deceives Adam but this Man has a wife, mother of all living men. Sin is not explained. Sinners, men and the serpent are described.

When prophecy ceased, apocalypticism appeared. It did not bring new insight into the living God. It had itself and its books to feed upon. It could not cope with the present, it projected its anxiety and its hope into the future. Judaism refused to canonize it, and Christianity, after initial temptations, chose the way pointed out by St Luke.

The New Testament authors themselves progressed in their theological achievements. Mark may have believed himself the narrator of past events. He was a commentator. So was St Luke, who knew but did not admit it. St Paul was not the first to reach the stage at which the speakers interpreted the data of the life of Jesus and of Old Testament passages in theological categories discovered or adopted by themselves. Therefore the hagiographers of the New Testament were in fact commentators of the revelation that was Jesus. Hence it is easier for us today to distinguish between what was observed by eye-witnesses and transmitted in tradition, and what is stated as a kind of anamnesis (even when apparently reliably historical in content and intention). Other

---

[11] Covenant thinking can be carried on in collective terms, but cannot avoid raising the problem of individual responsibility. Utilitarian-Sapiential thinking will define sin as foolishness. The religious genius of the prophet will see it as personal disobedience against a holy and merciful God.

New Testament theological statements are secondary to the witnessed, and later to the experienced mystery of Christ, and are elicited by it. Faith was in search of categories. The categories were found in the Old Testament. Key phrases were understood as prophecies and types of Christ. Thought patterns and precedents formed the narrative tradition.

It is a fact that certain topics and doctrines have a broad basis in Christian revelation; chronologically, geographically, theologically they are ubiquitous in the New Testament. The obvious examples are christology, the Eucharist and the law of love. Others appear in one clearly defined point in time and space: The primacy of Peter has a narrower base than the Infancy Narratives, the Feeding of the Multitudes a larger one than both. The isolated, clearly marked emergence of original sin in Paul is paralleled in its narrow basis perhaps only by the Petrine primacy. Both come from one passing point of time and place; both are accepted as part of a larger whole, as inspired as the respective writing itself. It is not difficult to admit that such doctrines could not have been parts of the common patrimony of the central message of Christianity. They were solutions of practical and concrete problems, theological or juridical or practical dilemmas solved on the spot. Once they are canonized, the Church has no power over the texts. But the exegete and the biblical theologian must never forget their origin. They are necessary logical complements of gaps that existed in the earlier tradition.

The final consideration relevant to the evaluation of the biblical doctrine of original sin is that of the relationship of sources and their use by the hagiographer. In many cases in non-narrative materials, the source-authority is used only as support for a doctrine already existing and arrived at by christological considerations. This is the case with the Pauline Old Testament proofs for doctrines such as justification by faith and original sin.[12]

II. St Paul

This principle is of crucial importance for St Paul's doctrine on Adam's sin. The doctrine's presence in Paul is not caused by his knowledge of Genesis, nor by his reliance on a Second Adam

[12] For a different view, see, e.g., De Fraine, *loc. cit.*, p. 133 f.

theology, but by the intellectual problem centred in the unique work of Jesus. Paul explains Jesus, not Adam. He discusses redeemed mankind, not the Adam of Genesis. In other words: the Second Adam theory is only a means to say something already known about Christ. It will be a great step forward if the exegete again has the courage to listen to Paul first and then to measure the distance Paul has travelled from his source. After all, he turned Abraham into a Christian (and James knew how "unscientific" this was). It is then more easily realized that the proper exegesis of Rom. 5 must not start with Genesis and its rabbinical exegesis available or not available, accepted, rejected, or modified by Paul, but by an obedient listening to his christology, by defining from his christology the exact size and function of the gap into which an adapted interpretation of Genesis and of a First Adam category was fitted. That Paul may have consciously thought he was learning from Genesis, and that he eagerly put to good use the authority of the word of God, does not invalidate the strength of the argument supported everywhere in Paul that his one starting-point is Jesus crucified and the revelation of the Lord.

Why Redemption? The first problem was the scandal of the Cross. St Paul answered it to his own satisfaction by recourse to the Old Testament, and thus joined Jesus himself, who did what was his Father's will. That mankind—that is, each individual who comes to faith—was redeemed from individual personal sins is the common answer of all Christians of the apostolic age. The Messiah came. Salvation is past, present and future. Mankind existed before Christ, and if a redemption had to take place there must have been a state out of which the believer himself was rescued, a state that must have been radically different from the pneumatic present. Beyond the concrete instances of the convert's forgiveness of sin and of the emergence of a body of Christ, the problem of the unredeemed past of mankind looms. If the term of redemption is to be in Christ as his body, might not the reality out of which the body of Christ is built have itself been superpersonal? A false reliance on the sources may again suggest that the "mystical body" is the replica of fallen anthropos or of collective Adam. Paul, in my opinion, first experienced that he lived in the body of Christ. Then he was driven by his own theology to catch a short glimpse of humanity "in Adam".

But how and why is mankind sinful? The simple answer first attempted by St Paul—"multiply individual sins until every single individual is an actual sinner"—was carried out with a ruthless logic, with Paul's characteristic inability to imagine concrete reality except in abstract words. He exploits the words of the whole Old Testament, and carries into the captivity of sin not only Israel but the whole Pagan World. Understood as a description of a real world and of real people, this is clearly false and monstrous. (Trent knew it to be so.) Understood as it was intended and experienced by Paul, it is the truth of God's holiness and of the Christian's dignity as the "new creation". If all pagans are sinners and if they have no law of Moses to violate, they must have violated their conscience. Both are still an amorphous conglomerate of individuals until, in "Adam", Paul is able to blame not only the individual as such but both Jew and Gentile together in their common ancestor.

History and the Old Testament now fail him. He had to disregard all the just in the same Genesis: all the prophets put to death for God's Word, all the good pagans of the Old Testament, and the obvious testimony of his senses. But he has found Adam, and in him a foil to Christ. If there is no other name to be saved by, but the name of Jesus, Adam (and in him mankind) cannot have that which is offered only in Christ.

If Christians are in Christ and the body of Christ, then mankind may also have been *en Adam* and *soma tou Adam*. Strangely enough, this is not asserted. This is another sign of the primacy of the Christ experience as a source of Pauline thought. But the limits are reached: Adam is *psyche zōsa*. Christ is *pneuma zoopoioun*. The rest of the mystery of evil in concrete persons is adequately handled by the word-pair *sarx-pneuma*.

III. JESUS AND JOHN

Speculation on original sin cannot have originated with Jesus. He does not mention the topic. His optimism concerning the powers of every individual of good will to do penance, and finally his image of God, all-powerful, all-merciful, now forgiving sin through Jesus, are the main indications that there is no place in the doctrinal system of Jesus for such a theological inquiry into the past.

Since the Master was silent on the origin of sin, the disciples—who did not have the intensity of Jesus' religious insight—necessarily fell back on their own resources, the Old Testament and contemporary Jewish thought. The concrete doctrine of Jesus, specific and restricted in applicability by its very concreteness and theocentricity, was soon applied—sometimes against its very nature—to new questions, less deep but more practical. In the matter of evil, such applications remained on the level of Old Testament solutions: God foresaw and foretold Israel's disobedience. The purpose of the parables now becomes concealment instead of the original invitation that respected human freedom. The parable of the sower becomes an allegory of the reasons for apostasy. It is not far from here to the revalued doctrine of the last judgment, to the problem of the presence of sinners in the Matthean Church, and to Paul's Adam the sinner.

Johannine theology is sacramental anamnesis of the incarnate Jesus. The *Kosmos* and its father, the murderer from the beginning, belong to the past as little as the Father of Jesus is a God of the past, as little as Jesus and the Paraclete are of the past. Yet the *Kosmos* is also the original object of God's love. Sinful *Kosmos* has a past, after Creation it must have had a beginning of sin. But it is subsumed into a timeless present in which the Logos of God, once incarnate in the *Kosmos*, now present in the Gospel, calls the world from darkness into light. This presence, and the call to decision that radiates from it, make an inquiry into the human past irrelevant for John.

A God of love beyond human comprehension, a God incarnate in Jesus Christ; St Paul, a man of limited but penetrating intelligence, a man who could really experience only the love of God revealing itself in Jesus Christ, a man who could see the past only in the light of the present: such are the factors that contributed to the New Testament doctrine of original sin, foreseen and sensed rather than intellectually understood.

Carl Peter

Original Sin: A Test Case in Theology

PAIN and suffering have plagued humanity throughout its history. What is more, men have asked themselves why there is evil in the world ever since they began to think systematically. Still, that something is wrong in the basic human condition is a proposition more readily admitted today than was the case even two decades ago.[1] In this context the biblical exegete and dogmatician have a remarkable opporunity to put their different types of expertise to work positively in man's collective efforts towards self-under-standing and improvement.

I. Evil in a World of Progress with Side-effects

The question they must apply themselves to is that of evil in the concrete present. What leads so many to near despair today is not that the world is imperfect or that there is evil in it. That is one thing. But why is there such evil that man's successes are far fewer than they might have been, and, even at that, why are they won only with the expenditure of far more effort than need have been? Not why evil of any sort, but why such utterly *excessive* evil as man encounters in himself and others?[2] It is this gnawing uncertainty that gives the problem of evil a greater force than ever in our day.

---

[1] Cf. Charles Moeller, "Fede cristiana e cultura contemporanea", *Fede e Mondo Moderno* (Rome, 1969), pp. 47–89.

[2] For a philosophical exposition of the problem, cf. Frederick Sontag, *God, Why Did You Do That?* (Philadelphia, 1970), pp. 172 ff.

One hundred years ago man had accomplished less in his striving to improve the quality of his existence. The presence of pain, suffering, and anguish was more plausibly explained as the inevitable price to be paid for living. This is not so easy today. Many diseases that were fatal at that time are so no longer today because of human ingenuity and effort; much discomfort that was considered unavoidable at that time is at present only a memory. And if this is not true for all men, at least one must say there is no theoretical reason why it cannot be. Then one might have argued that a subsequent condition of creation by a personal God would be the presence of some evil in the world. At present, however, such reasoning appears to be not false but simply beside the point. Man has succeeded in too many instances in mastering himself and his environment. Of course much remains to be done, but in comparison with what the situation was when he started, man has come a long way. Neither the fact of evil is in question, nor its necessity in some form or another in finite, changing being. But one who believes in a loving God finds himself asking how a God who *really* loves can be so *excessively* permissive of evil. Was all the difficulty that is connected with human achievement necessary for the pedagogical purpose of reminding man that he is but the image and not God? The cost of human progress—could it have been slightly less painful? If God is love, how is it that man succeeds so seldom, then with great effort, and often too late for the ultimate breakthrough to benefit many who could so have profited from an earlier one?

But the stubborn resistance offered by evil to man's mastery of the world is not the only problem. It is not as if each purposeful action of man reduced the area of the unknown and incalculable. The more he plans the more his knowledge extends to previously uncharted data. But simultaneously the realm of the incalculable is increased by the unforeseen and uncontrolled side-effects of his intervention.[3] Why do the consequences of his action on himself and his environment so often prove to be adverse to his own best interests?

In answer to this question, some men recur to chance, and others to the open future summoning humanity in the present

[3] Cf. K. Rahner, "Towards a Theology of Hope", *Concurrence* 1 (1969), p. 32.

tension of history to a not-yet in which antitheses other than those that are social will cease.[4] Both groups are engaged in a quest for the meaning of human existence and in so doing recur to a faith out of which a particular understanding of reality arises.[5] The Christian too has a faith-perspective, one that can and does lead to an understanding of the phenomenon of evil. To be of service to others, he must not remain silent regarding his convictions but must make an attempt today as never before to render an account of the hope that is in him.[6] Fidelity to God's word spoken in Jesus Christ requires more than silence; mere repetition of past expressions, however true, will not suffice for the needs of the present and future. That means concretely that the Christian must apply himself to the question why God chose a world where human survival and progress are possible, but only at the cost of such back-and-heart-breaking difficulty. Here, I submit, the dogmatician and biblical exegete find a promising point for their collaboration in an effort to articulate that fundamental aspect of the mystery of evil long designated as original sin.

II. Presuppositions and Method

Both begin their work within a cultural horizon that differs notably from those of the texts they deal with as theological specialists (the Scriptures and the faith experience of the Christian Church down through the centuries). Both also observe canons of scientific procedure that are equally applicable to the hermeneutics of secular documents from the past. Their faith unites them, of course; through it, they share in common a whole set of values they consider worth preserving, purifying, intensifying, and multiplying. Indeed, to varying degrees, but always positively, those values make themselves felt in the way both operate scientifically. Even in pure theory, if Christian faith is part of the religious and cultural horizon within which the exegete and dogmatician live, it would be difficult to imagine their failing to

[4] For an example of the latter, cf. E. Bloch, *Das Prinzip Hoffnung* (Frankfurt, 1959), pp. 1399 ff.

[5] K. Löwith, in the epilogue (pp. 206–7) to his *Meaning in History* (Chicago, 1970), points to the dilemma this same phenomenon poses for a reason that prefers not to believe.

[6] 1 Pet. 3. 15.

be influenced in any way by it in their critical thought and scientific endeavours. But, practically as well, they do in fact assume that the faith-experience witnessed to in the biblical tradition has a diagnostic value for the present as well, one that mankind will be better off for having had brought to bear than if the opposite were the case. The precise relation between the critical thought and the faith-commitment of each may vary. But to the extent that they theologize as Christians and particularly as Roman Catholics, they seek to understand the present and look to the future in the light of a particular, temporally determinable faith-tradition. This is done with a conviction that humanity is served if Christians bring their own religious-moral horizon into relation with that of their past, especially the apostolic age, so that violence is done to neither, both can converge, and the God active in each can speak his word of instruction, consolation, and encouragement for the future in the people and events of the present.

But how in fact do contemporary Catholic scholars in the fields of dogmatic and biblical studies assess the revealed word's meaning with regard to evil in the human condition? They do so in a recognizably and specifically Christian manner—a fact that should not be overlooked in the midst of undeniable disputes.

God created man with a real offer of friendship and union with himself. From the outset of his history, man has selfishly rejected the divine initiative with the lasting consequence of moral indigence in himself and the world he is born into. God's generosity has nevertheless endured and come to visible realization in Jesus Christ, whose Spirit inspires all men to overcome evil with good. That this is necessary for the Christian view of reality does not seem to be the issue in regard to original sin today.[7] There are also areas of disagreement: the type and extent of the symbolism employed by the biblical authors and the magisterium with regard to human origins; monogenism; and the moral evaluation of the religious situation into which man is born as member of a sinful race (In what sense is this situation sinful?).[8]

---

[7] Relative to man's *need* (my italics), for rebirth according to the Spirit, after birth according to the flesh (p. 107), cf. H. Haag's *Is Original Sin in Scripture?* (New York, 1969) (*Biblische Schöpfungslehre und kirchliche Erbsündenlehre*, Stuttgart, 1966).

[8] *Ibid.*

These matters of dispute are not unimportant. But one thing appears evidently clear from the present state of the question. Good will and theological expertise have not so far led to accord regarding some of the implications of man's need of redemption. Hence the following suggestion may have some merit.

There may be little hope for progress in understanding if theological specialists keep on asking themselves whether the *one man* of Rom. 5:12 ff., must be interpreted as one, and only one, instance of *homo sapiens* in the faith and understanding of subsequent generations of Christians; indeed, whether original sin is or is not found in Scripture. Answers to such questions depend on something else: the position one takes regarding the normative role of the Scriptures in Catholic thought and life.[9] Unless dogmaticians and exegetes come to better grips with this issue, there is real danger that both will set up straw men (perhaps valid enough even a few years earlier, but caricatures of their colleagues' positions today). This would mean they would do little positively to offer a credible option to other men anxious to know how Roman Catholics seek to understand their faith in regard to the evil in the world today. Perhaps, too, the area of disagreement will lend itself to more satisfactory treatment by exegete and dogmatician if they collaborate on the issue of a loving God in a world of staggering evil.

III. Analogues for God in a World of Needless Evil

For the Catholic Christian it comes as no surprise that man needs mental images to help him understand his belief in the loving Father of the Lord Jesus (D.S. 3016). But what is the analogue that is needed in a world of excessive evil?

The death-of-God theology levelled the charge of moral intolerability against the idea of a God who could but would not prevent evil.[10] Some might be tempted as a reaction to liken God to one who has two ears always open to listen and understand.

[9] Cf. R. Murphy and C. Peter, "The Role of the Bible in Roman Catholic Theology", *Interpretation* 25 (1971), pp. 77–94.

[10] My review of F. Sontag's *God, Why Did You Do That?* introduces some of the same considerations in the context of theodicy; cf. *The Thomist* 35 (1971).

Such an image has its advantages of course. It counters the wide-spread inclination to conceive of God as characterized by apathy in the depth of his transcendent, immutable being.[11] Even though man has in the meanwhile been forced by tragic circumstances to revise upwards his measure of the tolerable, this approach still has much to commend it to many. But for others (and I suspect their number is growing) such an approach does not help. A silent God, however supposedly concerned, interested, and sympathetic, will not do; things are too bad for that. For them, and for himself at times as well, the Christian needs more than this if his faith is to be credible.

His God, he says, is one who loves all men, and is not an aristo-crat who picks and chooses. Blind trust that the future will clear up the enigma of excessive evil does not render an account of Christian hope. But what kind of God is it who creates an unduly harsh world and still loves all?

The God and Father of Jesus Christ is one who loves not in our way but in his own, excessively and not by following some golden mean. His conduct and purpose need not involve choosing the shortest and easiest path for his creatures' self-fulfilment. A God of excessive love makes excessive evil in the world a credible chal-lenge that looks to a future testing of his promise that all will indeed end well. Recourse to such an image of God who says that he did all this because he wanted to is not an evasion of one's responsibility to say something about the here and now. It does not amount to a flight from the present as God-forsaken and offering no grounds for hope in a grace-filled future. Indeed it helps those who wait and work to do so not in total intellectual darkness but with a picture that makes reality presently intel-ligible and looks to the future for final verification.

The Christian Gospel and subsequent professions of faith pre-sent God as having loved excessively. The cross of Jesus was not the only way, the easiest way, or the shortest way to show that he who is the Father loves all men notwithstanding the evil they encounter, occasion, and cause. But that cross has from the start been understood and presented as a pledge that he who gave his

[11] For the patristic background, cf. W. Elert, "Die Theopaschitische Formel", *Theologische Literaturzeitung* 75 (1950), pp. 195–206.

only Son in excessive love is prepared to give men all things else as well (Rom. 8:31–2).

Of course Christian faith needs analogues to sustain it and keep it from evaporating into vague dreams. The one image suggested here is that of a God willing to answer the questions prompted by excessive evil in the world. This God does not appeal to pure reason as justification for what he has done. He has recourse to his own choice of world orders by a will strong enough, persevering enough, and caring enough to bring good out of evil not in a logic of proportion but in one of superabundance (Rom. 5:12 ff.). This image is intellectually respectable, and deserves to be taken more seriously in collaborative efforts of dogmaticians and exegetes when discussing original sin.

PART II
BULLETIN

Robert Ware

The Use of Scripture in Current Theology

HOW do theologians use the Bible? Examine several, and a classical handbook too, and discover for yourself how Scripture is used in the actual practice of theology. The backdrop of current usage is in the dogmatic handbooks which were still standard seminary texts on the eve of the Second Vatican Council. By and large these texts were a historical, dogma-centred presentations of "the teaching of the Church". Often—as in the ecclesiology of F. A. Sullivan[1] —this "teaching" was couched in the juridical and apologetic idiom of neo-scholasticism. The use of Scripture to corroborate dogmatic theses disregarded the logical character of biblical statements in their original context. At times, one sensed an athletic urgency to score enough biblical "points" to amass an "argument from authority" in support of the foregone conclusions and preconceived answers of dogmatic theses. This is of course a caricature —but for some, perhaps, a familiar one. Whereas medieval scholasticism understood itself in theory—but contrary to its actual practice—as a theology of conclusions, neo-scholastic theology was very often in fact and method a theology of dogmatic answers which used the Bible as a quarry of authoritative *dicta probantia* to legitimate the eternal truths of its conclusions. The extreme

[1] *De Ecclesia*. I. *Quaestiones Theologiae Fundamentalis* (Rome, 1963); cf. Y. Congar, "Christ in the economy of salvation and in our dogmatic tracts", *Concilium*, 1, n. 2 (London, 1966; American edn., vol. II; T. M. Schoof, *A Survey of Catholic Theology 1800–1970* (New York, 1970) (*Aggiornamento*, Baarn, 1968); W. Kasper, *The Methods of Dogmatic Theology* (New York, 1969) (*Die Methoden der Dogmatik*, Munich, 1967).

model of this "Denzinger theology", in my own memory, was a treatise *De Inspiratione* (S. Tromp?) still in use at Rome's Gregorian University in 1960.

Present-day theologians would surely be much more at home in assimilating the result of biblical scholarship, and much more sensitive to their own preconceptions. But to what extent would modern theologians' systematic and preconceptual background predetermine the questions they bring to Scripture, and the findings of their research? Are the questions perhaps already answers of a sort, as in the old catechisms or the bygone thesis-theology, or are they genuine research questions, opening perspectives for insight and learning? In this context, what does it mean to say a theologian must question the Bible "under the inspiration of the Church's actual consciousness of faith" (K. Rahner)? My own findings indicate that for lack of a better, the dogmatic background of neo-scholasticism (in a greatly changed context of course) continues to work quietly on in the methods and mentality of much contemporary theology. Hence, in retrospect, the one classical handbook examined, M. Schmaus, *Katholische Dogmatik* (Munich [4-5]1949–53),[2] proved surprisingly modern in its use of Scripture.

I. THE SUBJECT-MATTER OF THEOLOGY

The personal bias of academic training and familiarity with the literature led me to consider almost exclusively dogmatic or systematic theologians. In view of the unquestioned priority of systematic and dogmatic theology,[3] especially in the Roman Catholic tradition—though not exclusively there—I feel it is hardly necessary to justify this procedure.

As a point of departure I adopted D. H. Kelsey's distinction[4] of the inherent authority of Scripture (the content of revelation)

---

[2] Cf. W. Schweitzer, *Schrift und Dogma in der Oekumene. Einige Typen des heutigen dogmatischen Schriftgebrauchs* . . . (Gütersloh, 1953), pp. 24–52.

[3] Cf. N. Lohfink, "Text und Thema. Zum Absolutheitsanspruch der Systematik", *Stimmen der Zeit* 181 (1968), pp. 120–126.

[4] D. H. Kelsey, "Appeals to Scripture in Theology," *The Journal of Religion* 48 (1968), pp. 1–21.

from the relative authority of Scripture "authorizing" theological judgments. The latter relation can be *indirect*, enlightening religious understanding. Or it can be *direct*: Scripture is used in theological reasoning as data, the warrant for drawing conclusions, or as backing for the warrant. Where Scripture is used and how (the logical character and the unity of the Scripture used) depends, according to Kelsey, on a prior (non-biblical) decision about the subject-matter of theology. This all-important decision is grounded, it seems to me, not only in the indirect role of Scripture in the religious life of the theologian (Kelsey), but primarily in the dogmatic and systematic commitments of the theologian *and* his tradition.

An excellent example is K. Rahner. Though indebted to the systematic tradition of Heideggarian existentialist ontology, Rahner exhibits a characteristic Roman Catholic bent in his conception of the subject-matter of theology: "the Church's consciousness of faith".[5] This is like an ecclesiological version of R. Bultmann's commitment to the ontic state of the man of faith, and not surprisingly it predisposes Rahner toward questions of an apologetic (fundamental theology) and ecclesiological nature. To this must be added Rahner's commitment to a conceptual system so brilliant and powerful that it imposes its categories upon everything it considers, including the Bible. The occasional biblical data considered in his theological arguments, though precise and technically unassailable, are so much grist in his conceptual mill. Herein lies the greatest distance between Rahner's systematic theology and the thoroughly biblical theology of Bultmann.

Both, however, proceed from basically similar, anthropocentric points of departure. The object of reflection for both in the self-understanding inherent in the concrete happening of faith. For both, Scripture provides normative instances of the objectification of faith's response to God's self-communication in Jesus. But where for Bultmann the kerygmatic preaching of the Word is the point of access to the original testimony of Jesus, Rahner decides for the written testimony of the Bible within an authoritative

[5] K. Rahner, "Scripture and Theology", *Theological Investigations* VI (London and Baltimore, 1969), pp. 89–97 (*Schriften zur Theologie* VI, Einsiedeln 1965, pp. 111–120); *Id.*, art. "Bible. Theology", *Sacramentum Mundi* I (London and New York, 1968), pp. 171 ff.

tradition made actual in the living magisterium. Thereby, the priority he imputes to the Church's actual consciousness of faith tends to be identified with "the living magisterium" as the immediate norm of theology.

Perhaps this explains in part the acerbity of his argument with H. Küng over the latter's *Unfehlbar? Eine Anfrage* (Einsiedeln, 1970).[6] The subject-matter of Küng's theology is the structural life of the Church as measured by "the Gospel of Jesus Christ". Under the aegis of a Catholic *"sola scriptura"* Küng calls into question concrete ecclesiastical practices in the name of ecclesiological ideals. The discovery of "early Catholicism" in the New Testament understanding of ministry, apostolic succession and Church order and teaching serves as a fulcrum and court of appeal against the concrete functioning of doctrinal and disciplinary authority in the modern Church. In the light of the dogmatic idealism characteristic of conventional Catholic Church-consciousness, such idealistic pragmatism as Küng's must indeed seem like a massive challenge of the whole theological and teaching edifice.

Still another controversy—this one directed at Rahner—results in my opinion from a comparable misunderstanding. In his little book, *Cordula, oder der Ernstfall* (Einsiedeln, 1966), H. Urs von Balthasar reproaches Rahner for falling victim to the modern anthropological "system", which radically reduces love of God to love of one's fellow men in the sterile realm of conceptualism. There is a double protest here, against the reduction ("the identification"), and against the conceptualistic approach to faith. As an antidote to both, von Balthasar proposes *martyrium*, the readiness to die for the concrete conviction of one's faith; this is the "theopragmatic" criterion of faith and the only genuine response to the self-revealing love of God in Christ's Cross. This ever-greater love of God is the subject-matter of von Balthasar's theology. From this theocentric perspective, Rahner's attempt to situate the love of God integrally within the human context of love of neighbour appears to capitulate before "the system", although in fact the identification involves no reduction.

---

[6] In: *Stimmen der Zeit* 186 (1970), pp. 361–377 (Rahner); and 187 (1971), pp. 43–64, 105–122 (Küng).

All theologians today would allow that it is not the writing but the reality rendered which is ultimately decisive in the Scriptures. Yet much of even the best contemporary theology contents itself with speculative theological study of concepts, in the Bible as in later dogmatic tradition.[7] Furthermore, dogmatic perspectivism continues to be a most constricting selective factor. Thus, for example, B. Lonergan's course on christology focuses on the Incarnation, and betrays an Anselmian attitude towards Christ's crucifixion (disregard of resurrection); this predetermines the manner of raising questions about redemption. His failure to include more than a few incidental remarks about the Resurrection does violence to the christological perspectives of the New Testament.[8] Likewise, W. Pannenberg's ambitious programme of "revelation as history" is said to over-systematize the complex historical reality of the Old Testament, and even to turn a blind eye to scriptural data which are not germane to his programme.[9] Yet Pannenberg is remarkable among systematic theologians in that he controls at first-hand the exegetical material he uses, even when taken from the highly respected exegetes of the so-called "Pannenberg Circle" (R. Rendtorff and U. Wilckens).

It seems that the Scriptures render a fullness and depth of concrete reality which neither "teaching" nor systematic programme can contain. *Cordula,* cited above, makes very little "use" of Scripture, yet it seethes with an indignation rooted in a scriptural "sense" for the reality rendered in the Scriptures. We should dwell on this phenomenon, for it promises the possibility of passing beyond any mere "use" of the Bible, or "appeal" to Scripture, and the attainment of an integral "access" to the reality of Scripture.

[7] Cf. J. Barr, *The Semantics of Biblical Language* (London, 1961); *Id., Old and New in Interpretation* (London, 1966).

[8] Cf. G. O'Collins, "Thomas Aquinas and Christ's Resurrection", *Theol. Studies* 31 (1970), p. 514. For a survey of the christological handbooks of M. Schmaus, B. Lonergan, and A. Piolanti, cf. R. Lachenschmid, in: *Bilanz der Theologie im 20. Jahrhundert* III (Freiburg, 1970), pp. 83–84.

[9] C. Westermann, "Zur Auslegung des alten Testaments", in: O. Loretz & W. Strolz (Eds.), *Die hermeneutische Frage in der Theologie* (Freiburg, 1968), pp. 196 ff.; H. Waldenfels, *Offenbarung. Das II. Vatikanische Konzil auf dem Hintergrund der neueren Theologie* (Munich, 1969), pp. 106 f., 116.

II. THE "SPIRITUAL" USE OF SCRIPTURE[10]

Modern theology has been an historical dialectic between objec-tivizing and subjectivizing views of God, of faith and of the subject-matter of theology. In its recent form, the problem is frequently posed in terms of the respective theocentric and anthropocentric points of departure of K. Barth and R. Bultmann. But more is involved here than simply methodological questions of formal interpretation. Barth reputedly is liable for a biblical or revelation positivism which neglects the present historical situa-tion of man and his self-understanding. But the tremendous response to his *Römerbrief* suggests that in a very practical way he succeeded in speaking directly to the needs of his generation. This was due less to the content of his book than to the intense sincerity and integrity of his approach to Scripture. In sharp contrast to the impersonal methodological objectivity sought after in the history-of-religions school, Barth displayed an immediate religious access to Scripture and a personal ingenuousness forgetful of self and totally taken up with the content of revelation.

A similar note echoes in the following autobiographical state-ment: "I have always had a great love for Holy Scripture ... I was always struck by the fact that in my own theology studies, Scripture had been used primarily only as a means of demonstrat-ing theses which were already established. Consequently, I have consistently tried to think first in terms of Scripture and then to integrate the tradition and the dogmas into this perspective. This was pretty much of an unreflective process, of course, but it did serve to mature me for the critical reflection on a good bit of cur-rent theology, although on the other hand for a long time I con-tinued to examine dogmas in a rather fundamentalistic light, until the early sixties. ..."[11]

---

[10] "Spiritual" refers generally to the indirect role of Scripture for the religious understanding of the theologian, but also, specifically, to the kind of cultivated *"sens spirituel"* uncovered in the two major works of H. de Lubac, *Histoire et Esprit* (Paris, 1950), and *Exégèse médiévale*, 4 vols. (Paris, 1959–64).

[11] P. Schoonenberg, in: *The Crucial Questions on Problems facing the Church Today* (New York, 1969), pp. 112–113; cf. *Id., Hij is een God van mensen* (Hertogenbosch, 1969); *Id., Man and Sin. A Theological View* (London, 1965) (*De Macht der Zonde*; Hertogenbosch, 1962—revised);=

The actual use P. Schoonenberg makes of the Bible in his writing indicates that the primacy of Scripture in his theology is twofold: (a) the originally *pre-reflexive*, "spiritual" primacy of God's word in Scripture for the life of the Christian believer; (b) the *methodological* primacy of Scripture as the paradigmatic *norm* of theological interpretation. In the practical business of daily theology, however, the dogmatic concern is foremost and constitutes the subject-matter of his theology. His recent far-reaching christological essay, for example, is intended simply to be "a corrective and a completion" of the enhypostasis model of Chalcedon. He does check himself every step of the way against the biblical christologies of the New Testament. In his earlier essay on sin, commitments to dogma tradition, as the object of theological reinterpretation, and to theological (Rahner) and philosophic (Teilhard de Chardin) language and system often take the edge off Schoonenberg's pre-reflexive "spiritual" sense for the mind of Scripture. At times, too, the accumulation of biblical citations does not genuinely advance understanding. Both studies document Schoonenberg's dogmatic approach to theology and his "spiritual" use of Scripture.

His ingenuousness, grounded in prayerful listening to Scripture and its echo in dogma tradition, though it is far removed from the "objectivity" of much historical text criticism, is not pietistic. He combines individuality of thought with closeness to biblical idiom, a theological insight honed on the modern religious problematic and a methodology which respects the historical distance between the Bible and today. In the conversation cited above, Schoonenberg refers too to the liturgy as the prime bearer of orthodoxy in its thanksgiving prayer, to the insightful search of God in Ignatian spirituality, and to the "secularized" prayer life of young Jesuit colleagues as other elements influential on his own theological growth.

III. The Bible as Norm of Theology

It is indeed particularly in prayer and worship that genuine contact with Scripture was kept alive during periods of

Mysterium Salutis II (Einsiedeln, 1967), pp. 845–941); *Id.*, "God's tegenwoordigheid in Christus", *Tijdschrift voor Theologie* 9 (1969), pp. 375–405.

methodological *mis*use and *ab*use of the Bible. This spiritual aspect of the influence and use of Scripture in theology merits much closer attention than is possible here. For it is the normative methodological use of Scripture in the service of dogmatic commitments which is more characteristic of contemporary theology.

The Second Vatican Council has reinstated the Bible—in principle—as the norm for theology. But, like the call to the Bible as the "soul of theology" (*Dei Verbum*, n. 24), this is more a goal and an ideal than a statement of fact or a methodological principle. In the preparation of documents in the Council itself, especially the Dogmatic Constitutions, careful attention was given to the exegetical accuracy of the large number of Scripture citations. In the actual use of Scripture there were notable successes and notable failures.

The statement on the Jews, the final chapter especially of *Dei Verbum* on Revelation, and chapter 2 of *Lumen gentium* on the Church, are deeply imbued with a sense of Scripture and salvation history.[12] But the rational approach to man in the Declaration on Religious Freedom is singularly old-fashioned; there is no sign of a biblical vision of man in his relationship to God and to civil society. (The Bible passages cited to show the generosity of Jesus and his followers to those who disagreed with them, though well-meaning, are patronizing in this context and serve only as illustrative data in a completely rational argument.) Similarly, notwithstanding revolutionary progress in the systematic understanding of revelation in *Dei Verbum,* the maintenance of the triumvirate Scripture, Tradition and Magisterium as three discrete entities in chapter 2 reveals how little conventional dogmatic commitments have been subjected to the perspectives of Scripture. The Bible continues to provide data to explicate God's word today, but all too often only as a paraphrase or an outline of conceptual relationships in biblical literature.

The ambiguities evidenced in conciliar practice have not been

---

[12] From the vast literature on the Council documents, in addition to H. Vorgrimler (Ed.), *Commentary on the Documents of Vatican II*, 5 vols. (New York, 1967–69) (*Das II. Vatikanische Konzil*, 3 vols., Freiburg, 1966–1968), cf. G. Baum, in *Ecumenical Theology*, No. 2 (New York, 1967), pp. 211–239, 247–272; O. Loretz, "Die hermeneutischen Grundsätze des II. Vatikanischen Konzils", in: O. Loretz & W. Strolz, *op. cit.*, pp. 467–500; H. Waldenfels, *op. cit.*

remedied since its conclusion. The bewildering variety of approaches to Scripture at present is amply illustrated in three test-cases presented by C. Peter:[13] the diversity of Church orders in the New Testament, the human knowledge of Jesus and the problem of evil. For E. Schillebeeckx and H. Küng the New Testament diversity constitutes a norm of non-exclusion keeping the future open and legitimating a plurality of Church orders. For Y. Congar and M. Bourke the New Testament indicates rather a positive line of development giving normative direction and specificity to the future. R. E. Brown's middle position seeks unity of belief and consistency in witness as the biblical norm. The negative norm is again evident in K. Rahner's christology, where exegetical results preclude certain systematic conclusions regarding the perfection and extent of Jesus' knowledge and freedom. On the other hand, systematic constructs (e.g. the supernatural existential) central to his thought are less critically founded in Scripture. B. Lonergan is an example of the movement from analysis of human consciousness, knowledge and spontaneity to a deeper appreciation of biblical texts. Finally, P. Schoonenberg moves from the biblical conception of social solidarity in sin to an original statement of the problem of evil, while M. Flick and Z. Alszeghy proceed in the opposite direction from criticism of dogmatic theories to biblical discovery. These examples document the lack of any operational consensus in the actual practice of theologians with respect to the use of Scripture as norm.

A final, negative example reflecting the *status quo ante* shows how far even official Church documents in the post-conciliar period fail in practice to rise to the goal of Vatican II. Pope Paul VI's encyclical on Priestly Celibacy[14] contains 110 biblical citations. But there is neither biblical reflection as such nor evidence of exegetical evaluation. In fact, the citations would not be missed if omitted. Contrary to the standards of *Dei Verbum* (n. 12), all citations possess equal speculative and dogmatic value, yet they are insufficient to demand celibacy or even to provide it with

[13] C. J. Peter, in: R. E. Murphy and, "The Role of the Bible in Roman Catholic Theology", *Interpretation* (Jan. 1971), pp. 87–94.

[14] *Sacerdotalis Caelibatus* (Rome, 1967); cf. A. Antweiler, *Zur Problematik des Pflichtzölibats der Weltpriester. Kritische Erwägungen zur Enzyklika* ...(Münster, 1968), pp. 55–72.

post-factum biblical foundation and meaning. Thus the objection that compulsory celibacy for priests cannot be grounded in the New Testament (n. 5) is rather confirmed than refuted by the encyclical's pious biblical reminiscences.

The present state of theology, methodologically, with respect to the Bible, warrants the claim that exegetical findings have little or no relevance for the dogmatic basis for doing theology. In 1962 E. Schlink published a report on interconfessional discussions (±90 papers since 1946) which revealed a surprisingly far-reaching agreement in exegetical findings, but incomparably greater diversity with respect to dogmatic theology: "In a word, the frightening finding is the relative meaninglessness of the consensus of biblical exegesis for the mutual relationship of both parties' dogmatic statements".[15] This pre-conciliar judgment has lost little if any of its actuality. It is not enough to profess allegiance to formal methodological priorities when these are not implemented in actual functional operations.

Among first-generation, post-conciliar theologians who appeal extensively to the normative authority of Scripture, one of the most popular and controversial is H. Küng.[16] A dogmatic theologian, an ecclesiologist, an ecclesiastical polemicist event ("*Kontroverstheologe*"!), Küng depends exclusively upon the exegetes for his biblical material. Though he cites a wealth of literature in his writing, he collates material more than he integrates it in an original synthesis. Küng is capable of critical discussion with the exegetes. But, at times, he is less critical about accepting in their conventional form points of departure and formulations of a problem. The notion "originality" is an example: distinguishing chronology, authenticity and relevance, Küng uses it as a basis for evaluation and selection. In conjunction with "early Catholicism" it further serves as a warrant for a sort of Catholic "*sola scriptura*". Yet the status of the concept itself is not adequately

---

[15] E. Schlink, "Pneumatische Erschutterung?", *Kerygma und Dogma* 8 (1962), pp. 221–237; cit. p. 228.

[16] Cf. H. Küng, *Structures of the Church* (London, 1964), pp. 135–151 ("early Catholicism") (*Strukturen der Kirche*, Freiburg, 1962); *Id.*, "Der Frühkatholizismus im NT als kontroverstheologisches Problem", *Kirche im Konzil* (Freiburg, 1963), pp. 124 ff.; *Id.*, *The Church* (London, 1967), pp. 15–24 ("originality") (*Die Kirche*, Freiburg, 1967); *Id.*, "Was ist die christliche Botschaft?", *Publik* (2 Oct. 1970).

secured. Is it not plausible even that later developments are more faithful expressions of the Spirit of Christ than their New Testament origins initially warranted?

A similar criticism can be made of Küng's appeal to "the Gospel of Jesus Christ" as the fundamental norm of his practical apologetics. This conception as he uses it is abstract, idealistic, and too little founded—Küng's undeniable intention—in the rich historical detail of Scripture. Even when spelled out (as in his talk at the Brussels *Concilium* Congress), its relation to the rest of his theology is not immediately evident. Therefore his conclusions, in the absence of a theory of practice which would warrant the theological move from biblical data to current ecclesiastical policy,[17] appear foreordained by the context of Church politics. Much confusion is dispelled if we take "the Gospel of Jesus Christ" to be a signature for specific scriptural backing to a pragmatic theological warrant. As it stands, Küng's use of Scripture is hamstrung by his own polemic intent to re-establish evangelical priorities and perspective in the current situation.

IV. "The Soul of Theology"?

It is becoming more and more imperative to redefine the priority and pre-eminence of Scripture, not merely as authoritarian norm and court of appeal, but as paradigmatic content for the experience of faith and the practice of theology.[18] The very pragmatic dilemma, Bible studies or systematics, in many a theology faculty, is false *in principle*. All theology that merits the name must be biblical theology directly or indirectly. Yet the integration of the Bible into systematic theology, excellent in concept, is in fact a Pyrrhic victory for a biblical theology, for the very simple reason that the vast majority of systematic theologians and dogmaticians

---

[17] Cf. D. H. Kelsey, *loc. cit.*, p. 17 f.; J. Moltmann, "Toward a Political Hermeneutics of the Gospel", *Union Seminary Quarterly Review* 23 (1968), pp. 303–323.

[18] Cf. W. Pannenberg, "The Crisis of the Scriptural Principle", *Basic Questions in Theology* (London, 1970), pp. 1–14 (*Grundfragen systematischer Theologie*; Göttingen, 1967, pp. 11–21); F. J. Schierse (answering G. Dautzenberg), *Was hat die Kirche mit Jesus zu tun? Biblische Exegese und kirchliche Verkündigung* (Düsseldorf, 1969); N. Lohfink, *loc. cit.*

are not adequately equipped to work or even think according to Scripture. Nor are these available concrete operational canons for the implementation of this goal. Perhaps the best that can be hoped for the time being is the merciless but constructive criticism of the biblical experts. My impression, however, is that most exegetes have been too long under strict dogmatic control and tutelage, and themselves require an apprenticeship in a theory of biblical practice which must still be written.

Here especially, the theological epistemology of J. B. Metz's "political theology" and J. Moltmann's "political hermeneutics" can play an important role, along with recent efforts to integrate the insights and logical rigour of linguistic analysis into theology.[19] Perhaps also Y. Congar's suggestion should be considered more earnestly, that every theologian in the course of his training be required to write at least one serious piece of biblical research. An exemplary work in this respect—"a systematic theologian at the school bench of the exegetes"— is K. Lehmann's exhaustive study of the confession formulas: "on the third day, according to the Scripture".[20] O. Loretz further proposes an independent Papal Biblical Commission to co-ordinate the results of biblical research in the service of an authentic teaching office based on expertise instead of control.[21] Preaching the Gospel is the primary magisterium of the Church—yet it defies imagination to conceive the mien of established Catholic teaching, if as much concern were shown for the accuracy *and* adequacy of Scripture in Church documents and theology as has been exercised towards maintaining the purity of dogmatic traditions.

Today all Christian conferences are faced with a Scripture crisis, and therein a crisis in their relationship to Jesus and the Father. Most have sought to resolve their difficulties theologically by an intellectual return to the sources of the traditions and by an

---

[19] J. B. Metz, "Religion and Society in the Light of a Political Theology", *Harvard Theol. Rev.* 61 (1968), pp. 507–523; J. Moltmann, *loc. cit.*; L. Gilkey, *Naming the Whirlwind: The Renewal of God-Language* (Indianapolis, 1969).

[20] K. Lehmann, *Auferweckt am dritten Tag nach der Schrift* (*Quaest. Disp.* 38) (Freiburg, 1968).

[21] O. Loretz, *loc. cit.*, pp. 486–491; cf. R. E. Brown, "Rome and the Freedom of Catholic Biblical Studies", in: J. M. Meyers e.a. (Eds.), *Search the Scriptures* (Leiden, 1969), pp. 129–150.

analysis of contemporary forms of thought. These attempts are less and less convincing, and suspicion is increasing that perhaps they have been conceived within the too narrow confines of conventional Christianity.[22] Notwithstanding a feverish desire to read the so-called signs of the times, by far the majority of contemporary theologians of all specialisms still theologize under the conceptual and normative presuppositions of an exclusively Church culture and tradition. This necessarily implicates them in an unnatural Church-world duality. The only questions today are secular questions; this includes *the* single most important secular question: the quest for ultimate meaning in an absolutely relative world—for theology, the God-question. It is indispensable that the questions be posed, and the quest be undertaken, in their present, so-called "secular" form, and not in the conventional form of a bygone Church world.

Perhaps H. Urs von Balthasar is right about the theo-pragmatic readiness to give up everything. His protest calls to mind Gandhi's demand that his followers be prepared to die (literally!) for the "truth-force" of militant non-violence (*satyagraha*), but also, in the service of Christian inspiration and Gandhian method, Martin Luther King's exemplary fulfilment of *martyrium*—and too, in another context, with another method, Camillo Torres. *This, too, is use of Scripture.*[23] But where are the exegetes who can instruct us from Scripture in political responsibility for social, economic, military and political violence and revolution? Theologians tend to rely on Scripture only for data, and this "causes theology to shirk its critical responsibilities and to turn into a paraphrase of Scripture", even though the Bible itself gives abundant backing to a warrant for theological judgments based upon data from the immediate situation.[24]

"Ascetic Christianity called the world evil and left. Humanity is waiting for a revolutionary Christianity which will call the

[22] W. H. van de Pol, *The End of Conventional Christianity* (New York, 1968) (*Het einde van het conventionele christendom*; Roermond, 1967); but especially: L. Dullaart, *Toekomst of traditie. Een kritiese dokumentatie over theologie, kerk en godsdienst* (Deventer, 1970).

[23] Cf. M. L. King, Jr., "Pilgrimage to Nonviolence", *Strength to Love* (New York, 1964), pp. 165-173; further, E. Erikson, *Gandhi's Truth. On the Origins of Militant Nonviolence* (London, 1969).

[24] D. H. Kelsey, *loc. cit.*, pp. 17 f.

world evil and change it".[25] This, as King and Torres rightly understood, is not a matter of retrospective idealism, but of prophetic inspiration and pragmatic methods. In place of an authoritarian-normative use of Scripture, perhaps we might try to implement a "truth-force" approach—at once a new spirituality *and* a new pragmatism. Instead of seeking mainly to explain and understand conceptually, we might try first to cross over to Jesus' standpoint before God (and to other biblical standpoints before God).[26] Perhaps then it will be possible to understand—to stand-under—the power of Scripture to change our lives and initiate action.

[25] W. Rauschenbusch, *Christianity and the Social Crisis* (New York, 1964), p. 91.

[26] Cf. J. S. Dunne, "The Human God: Jesus", *Commonweal* 87 (1967), pp. 508–511; *Id.*, *A Search for God in Time and Memory* (New York, 1969).

Jacques Audinet

The Banquet of Scripture:
The Bible and Adult Catechesis

"And there was this fantastic table in front of me with marvellous food on it and fresh helpings being brought all the time. So they told me about it and went through the menu, and invited me to help myself. But no one ever said why the table was there" (extract from an interview).

An exhaustive assessment of the role of the Bible in adult catechesis would be an impossible task. Even the phrase "adult catechesis" is far too vague. One knows what is involved in the catechesis of children or adolescents: in spite of changes it still remains bound up with institutions or techniques. But what about adult catechesis?

The expression is quite recent. For a time it was confused with the catechumenate, but quite soon a clear distinction was made between the two. It cannot be defined by reference to specific institutions or activities. In fact, it includes any effort to transmit the faith to the people of God or to communicate the faith within the people of God: in short, ordinary catechesis, the word in general, with no connection with any special organization or procedure. But giving such a broad definition means abandoning the attempt to say anything at all precise—whoever could hope to say how the Bible is taught, lived and prayed today? Nevertheless, something is definitely happening to the Bible. The way in which it "circulates" within the Christian and human communities is changing. Symptoms can be seen, both inside and outside the Churches. Can we try to interpret them and see what demands they embody, so that not only the banquet of Scripture is prepared, but those who eat know why?

1. Scripture has ceased to be a restricted book. It is no longer the private property of the Christian community. It circulates freely in contemporary culture, and is no longer subject to the control of the Churches.

For centuries the barriers of language and power made Scripture a source book, but access to it was reserved to, and controlled by, clerics. What the Reformation proclaimed has since become a fact on a much larger scale, thanks to modern communication media: large-circulation magazines, radio and television broadcasts, the literary press and so on[1] ensure that our contemporaries hear the Bible discussed regularly in sources other than the preaching of their churches. No doubt it will be argued that the position is different in each country, that there is an Anglo-Saxon tradition of promoting the Bible which is different from the Latin one, and that, of course, the success of these publications or films depends on their ambiguous reliance on an old Christian basis of religious awareness which can still arouse interest in that sort of thing. It is nevertheless true that the Bible is promoted, presented and read apart from the community of faith and those who exercise authority in it. This situation may be called "secularization", or post-Christian atheism, but it does not alter the fact that it is no longer possible to act as if the word were addressed to a public which had never heard it, or as if a knowledge of the faith could be taken for granted.

Such a dissociation of Scripture and faith, and of Scripture and Church, weakens one view of catechesis. Catechesis was not only the transmitting of the message, but a power which in practice reserved to itself the interpretation of that message. It was impossible to receive Scripture except through the authority of the Church accepted in faith. In a world considered Christian or, more precisely, Catholic, the three terms implied each other and it was impossible to separate them.

[1] This shift in the "locus" of the Bible in contemporary culture is the subject of an excellent study by P. Gritti, in *Bible et Techniques de Masse* (Paris, 1970). It is a comparative study of four recent documents, "At that time the Bible", "The Bible today" and "The Illustrated Bible" in *France-Soir*, and "The Bible" in *France Dimanche*. His investigation is rigorous, and uses a certain number of concepts from communications theory.

When it had become impossible to ignore the evidence that the situation had changed, and, in particular, that faith could be lacking in those who came into contact with Scripture, even through sermons, the first reaction was to maintain the familiar model: Church-faith-Scripture. Biblical catechesis is only for those who have the faith. At the very most, it was considered possible to use certain passages of the Old Testament in what was known as pre-catechesis.[2] But it is no longer possible to maintain so purist an attitude. The Bible is everywhere; it has become a consumer commodity. Preachers and catechists are in no position to restrict it to believers in the context of the preaching of the faith. No more are they in a position to influence the order or manner in which questions are raised. They arrive in bulk, depending on whatever issues are current: vital questions mixed in with points of detail. And they are associated with elements of explanation which owe nothing to the Bible or to tradition.[3]

In short, not only is the use of Scripture no longer the prerogative of the Churches, but even its interpretation is escaping their control. We have seen the Bible swept up in the flood of contemporary consumer culture and reduced to the common denominator of mass media's simple ideas or crude symbols. Does this mean that in leaving the specialists' ghetto it has lost only its identity? For a moment there was hope: the Bible would be promoted, and communicated to all, by the powerful tools of modern technology. Disappointment followed. It seems impossible at the same time both to make Scripture widely available, and to ensure that correct knowledge and interpretation of it are equally widespread. The Scripture scholar hesitates: is he to spread a message which will soon get out of his control, or to keep the keys in the name of truth and be condemned to silence?

[2] It is instructive to look at a few publications from the early period of the catechetical movement. See especially "La Bible, Histoire du Salut", *Lumen Vitae* X (1955), "Bible et Catéchèse, *Catéchèse* 3 (1961) and the various reports of successive *Congrès d'enseignement religieux*, which all give prominence to "teaching the Bible". The difference between these and recent publications is striking. One example of a recent publication is "Lettre aux communautés chrétiennes", *Bimensuel*, Centre National de l'Enseignement Religieux, Paris.

[3] Gritti has excellent examples. See *Bible et Techniques de Masse*, Chapter VII, p. 161.

But, by escaping from the Churches, Scripture appears more clearly in the other aspect as a part of the common cultural heritage of mankind. Read with different eyes, it finds its place in the human venture. Compared with today's stars, biblical heroes do not inevitably lose all interest or identity. Perhaps this could even be a way for Scripture to win a different sort of authority which it has within itself: that of a text which touches the essence of man and his questionings.[4] Now part of humanity, Scripture brings humanity something from without.

But it is the task of the Churches, of the preachers, of the catechists, to take a note of this new situation. What the Church says about the Bible is now only one voice among others. It must set itself up as one research centre among others. Is it possible for preachers and catechists to say something original, for the voices with which they bear witness to be specific and make known the Church's unique message about the Bible?

2. In the Christian community, Scripture has ceased to be a text which is listened to; the Bible is becoming a book which is read. The text has changed its function. This is particularly true of small communities. This aspect of the situation is complementary to the first. While the Bible spreads more and more beyond the limits of the Christian communities, within their limits its role is changing.

The liturgical reform has aroused a new interest in the texts as a result of the change to the vernacular and the universal availability of the texts. They are now no longer heard in an unknown language, or even listened to in translation, but spoken in the everyday language which is now also the language of the liturgy. They are not only spoken, but are much more easily available to all than in the past, when only an élite had access to them.

But, here too, enthusiasm has been followed by disappointment. The faithful Christian finds himself divided between, on the one hand, a desire to hold on to these texts, which he knows by faith are saying something to him, and, on the other, the difficulty he

---

[4] "Surely a humanity in the highest degree, in the agony of its relations with God, is one dimension of the biblical message? If so, it is interesting that it is also written into our present mass culture." (Gritti, *Bible et Techniques*, p. 188.)

experiences in finding any sustenance in them. Indeed, it is almost as though the texts lost their meaning for many people once they were stripped of their solemnity, and presented in their own right rather than through a preacher's commentary. The situation is even more striking in small groups. Often discussion gets bogged down or dries up. Instead of the expected treasure and living water, the reality is empty and arid.

Perhaps we have to realize that the texts, without changing in themselves, have changed their function. The deep springs to which they appealed are no longer the same. The liturgy as the place of the mystery, in some cases all the more evocative because it relied on a sacred atmosphere of incomprehension and silence, has been replaced by a liturgy which is a place of communication and requires in the first instance knowledge and expression.

In the solemn assembly, which brought together considerable numbers of people, the proclamation of the text had a unifying and activating role. The text was listened to according to a precise ritual. It was expounded in a homily or sermon which conformed to a fixed style, and—if we are to believe the sermon manuals of not very long ago –the word of the preacher was the sign of the transcendence of the word of God. This of course explains why no expression by the faithful was required, provoked or even tolerated. The texts and commentaries tried to be spiritual and universal, and the criterion of spirituality and universality was their fidelity to the teaching of the Church, which the whole audience accepted—or were presumed to accept.

When preaching changed its style, when it tried to be "relevant", "related to life", in touch with men's questions, it tried to be a sign of closeness rather than a sign of transcendence. From that time its function changed, and the function of the text changed with it. How could the text arouse the community and bring it to life when the effect of the word set forth in this group of people could only be to reveal the diversity of their questions? The point of reference was now not so much the teaching of the Church, presumed to be accepted in its entirety by all, as the view of the individual speaker. In this situation it was natural to claim the right to reply. But the attempt to adapt the word of God and make it more accessible to the assembly risked destroying its unity in the absence of any ability to place it on the required level.[5]

The position is different in small groups. Here the right of reply exists, and is even in a way primary since each member reads the text and gives his own commentary, or puts his own questions, or asks for those of the group. (The forms are unimportant, and vary widely.) Unity is no longer sought in a single view of the text but in the acceptance of different views. Expression is more important than reception, and the incantatory role gives way to a critical function.

One could draw up a typology of this criticism. There would be three levels. The first is that of history. At the same time as exegetes are worrying over the limits of the historical method, which has been their main instrument for over a century, Christian people are discovering a text and accounts of events, whose first requirement for credibility, in their view, is that they should "tell it as it was". Catechesis cannot do without this approach, but it cannot stop there. The historical approach to the text is a necessary preliminary for a genuine encounter with the text, and essential if one is to avoid an anecdotal or magical view of the Bible, but on its own it leads to a dead end. This has been the bitter discovery of many catechists who have tried this approach with children and adolescents. Apart from the fact that it requires in the leader a competence and knowledge which not everyone has, adult groups at least have the advantage that they soon realize that they are looking for something else, and that they want something from Scripture beyond "what happened", even when it has been expertly explained on the basis of "the results of the latest scholarship".

This leads to the second level, the moral approach to Scripture.

_____

[5] "Sunday Mass is very artificial. Especially in the sort of liturgy you get at High Mass. There has been a marked development in the last two or three years, but it's still very anonymous. What annoys me most of all about this type of liturgy is that there's no right to reply. It's a liturgy for people with nothing to say, the people sit there and they listen. . . ." (From an interview.) The change of intention on the part of the speaker leads to a change of function in what is said, and the results may be different from what was expected. It is a very urgent problem today to find a living word for large groups which is neither the pure objectivity of doctrine nor the subjectivity of the preacher.

"Looking for lessons from the Bible" is in one sense a traditional approach: this book, these texts, have something to teach us. But whereas the traditional preacher knew more or less what he had to find in Scripture, because accepted doctrine gave him a framework, today the opposite is very often true. The gap between Scripture, contemporary experience and the traditional formulation of accepted doctrine is obvious and seems to be widening. The liberation of the word has the effect, with Scripture as with everything else, of cancelling its immunity from questioning. It is impossible to turn Scripture into a book of convincing lessons. Either it becomes a pretext for a teaching which is not scriptural, or it points another way.

Many Christians are led by their desire to read Scripture to adopt a poetical approach—the realization that something is being said which is outside history or moral instruction: a unique experience which is at the same time that of men of the past and our own. It is an approach which goes beyond, and also comes before, that of commentaries which bring out the meaning or draw lessons. A "mystical approach", "lectio divina", in which the adjectives don't really matter.

The function of the text is changing. People are trying to tap an experience. This is one of the reasons why Scripture is often abandoned and tentatively replaced by other texts, and the search for a deep common experience, or for an experience which gives something. But an attempt at this kind of approach involves anxiety for any group. The fear of illusions, the recurrence of models from the past and the awkwardness felt about religious expressions, are among the most frequent obstacles.

Perhaps the only way of approaching Scripture today is for Christian groups, on the basis of a shared culture, to develop one or more specific approaches which go beyond history and try to reach the unique experience of which this book is the bearer. We must try to see what this involves

What role can there be for preachers and catechists in such a situation, in which they can no longer control the distribution and reading of Scripture? The food is ready on the table, but so many other tables are prepared. Is it a choice between trying to make ours look like the others at the risk of losing the substance, or cutting ourselves off from contemporary movements at the risk of death? Is there any other way?

1. Before dealing with any questions of method, one question arises immediately: Why? Why does the Church refer to Scripture? Why does it claim to give an authentic interpretation of Scripture and base its faith on the Bible? In a different age, when horizons were limited by the strict social control which placed unsurmountable barriers between the Christian and what was non-Christian, there was no need to justify the use which the Church made of Scripture. Or, more accurately, it was easily done once and for all. Once it had been said that the Bible was an inspired book and that the Gospel came to us from Christ and his disciples, there was no need to add anything else. The books drew their authority from this origin, which also justified the use the Church made of them and the control it exercised over that use.

But today the question "Why?" keeps coming up. Why do I, a Christian of the twentieth century, have to judge my faith by the standard of a word spoken or written centuries ago? Why, particularly when it is a word so often enigmatic and only to be made intelligible by such an amount of historical work that it becomes utterly remote from me? Or if I accept it in faith, is it not ultimately I who give this word its meaning, and so what use is it? Doesn't it really take a sort of archaic fidelity to penetrate to the meaning of Scripture? And if we get rid of this archaism or this eccentric interest in vanished civilizations, wouldn't it be more useful to try to build up our faith with the aid of different texts, modern ones which are more accessible and therefore more real? Couldn't we have a liturgy with readings from Camus or some other modern author?

The search for the origins is no longer enough. What began as explanation has become the problem; it is no longer enough to call a book inspired, the witness of the apostles. At the most this gives it the right to the respect due to an ancient relic, but not the binding force given to it by the practice of the Church. The assertion of a link with a revelation or a history is not enough; it is where the question arises. Accepting Scripture basically means accepting a link with a revelation given, a history which accomplishes something absolutely essential for my life today. "Why Scripture?" leads to the basic question, "Why faith? And why an historical and revealed faith?"

Is it possible to discern in Scripture at least the basis of an answer to this question? After all, is not the scriptural tradition a constant interaction between the present and what was given to "our forefathers" in the past? This means that to discover Scripture today is to discover what was given and the way in which it was given, in a unique historical tradition which was also a people's tradition of faith.

A word was spoken, and continues to be spoken. It is the words which are added to the first word which are its living extension. In reading Scripture and trying to transcribe it into any system (and this is where one rediscovers the old idea of the unity of Scripture), this unique and varied life of the tradition of the people of God is my object and absolutely essential to my faith. It is essential because faith is a link with a people and, through that people, with salvation brought by Jesus Christ. There should now be no surprise that Scripture is different and strange to us. It is the strangeness of any man to any other man; only as a result of their shared difference can communication take place. The word spoken in the past is a concrete, "incarnate" word, always spoken again in the fidelity of the living word.

In this sense, the reception of Scripture is quite different from commentary, and the Church's activity is not repetition. Christianity is the religion not of the incantation but of the incarnation of the living word. It is the bearer of an original approach to this book, one among the many approaches which can be made to it, and the endless explanations to which it gives rise and always will give rise. It is like visiting a church—a different experience depending on whether it is disused or still a place of worship. Who will ever know what it was like to listen to the Maya or Babylonian priests? We can attempt to reconstruct the experience out of ruins and documents, but they are the dead remains of dead experiences. Reading Scripture must produce more than the remnants of an experience. In this sense, exegesis which was no more than positive would fall short of what the Church expects. At a time when all disciplines are worrying about the boundaries between the scientific and the human we must go beyond the historical approach, not avoiding it but taking it further. We must read this human book in the most human way possible, with that of which it is the bearer, the highest of all human experiences, the meeting with God's salvation.[6]

2. It is this anxiety constantly to bring to life the question "Why?" which will inspire the question "How?", in reading, preaching or commentary. Too often, these get bogged down precisely because the function they pursue is not clear. People read, argue and expound, without any longer knowing why. What was the means, history, becomes an end which hides the real end. The object of the search, the food of life, is made more difficult to find by the operation of something different—the moralistic apparatus which is being surreptitiously reintroduced. The fundamental reason for reading Scripture must banish that. The real questions raised by the living word uncovered in a unique and original way must lead beyond story-telling or historical details as well as beyond casuistry. Today we have to discover how to go about this mystical and poetical approach.

How are we to teach Scripture? Educational research has given us abundant material on this point in recent decades. With the abandonment of fundamentalism and its rote-learning, the aids were "to make them understand", "to adapt", "to interest", "to go from the fact to the mystery", "to give meaning to experience", "to connect Scripture with life", "to recover a biblical outlook", and so on. At one time or another all these expressions were the slogans of biblical catechesis. The result is familiar: the preacher or catechist caught between the two terms of these expressions, and unable to make more than an awkward connection. More often than not one was sacrificed to the other. Either Scripture became a vague point of reference juxtaposed at all costs with a description of contemporary life, experience or events, or the other things were there really only as a pretext to "get across" something quite different. Catechesis saw the defeat of concordism. This can be seen also in the irritation of congregations at preaching unable to talk about God because it wants to talk about man or, conversely, wanting to talk about God but unable to do so except in a language so remote that it is impossible to tell whether transcendence is the result of anachronism or reality.

[6] Cf. Mircea Eliade, *The Quest* (Chicago, 1969), which offers rich reflections on the relations between historical methods and religious experience.

We are looking for a different way, a *"lectio divina"* for our time. Without claiming to describe it, we may be able to list its emphases. The starting-point is Scripture. The Bible is given. It is part of Christian existence. In Scripture the people find the tradition which gave it shape. Scripture bears witness to what we have received and what we live by. No apologetics will let us slip in references to texts and experiences which were not there from the beginning. In this experience, which is both human and religious, there is no dualism at the start—but the uniqueness of the biblical experience, its being at once human and divine. Listening to Scripture, preaching, commentary, questions, explanation (and these are different approaches) will come in only to allow those who are there to make this experience their own, and to see in the text they have received from tradition what enables them to live out the same adventure to-day. We are not dealing with a dead text, an archaic relic, a treatise or a manual, nor even with a history (or story) book. Scripture is simply there, constituted as holy Scripture by the same process by which the people assembled constitute them-selves the people of God. The same relation constitutes both; there would be no Bible without a people to read it who were initially the people who wrote it, and there would be no people without a memory to go on reviving what was given.

This basis, like any immediate experience, allows full scope for all the forms of interpretation which man can employ in his attempt to understand himself and reality: historical interpreta-tion, essential today for anyone who seriously wants to come to grips with documents which belong to the past while having a bearing on contemporary life, ethical interpretation, looking for norms and rules of conduct, symbolic interpretation, sensitive to basic attitudes and deep resonances and to the sense of the "beyond".

These various interpretations are often in conflict, and will shatter the first simple appreciation of the text. None of these interpretations is total, and no word is absolute. Rather, it is their interaction and the reference of each to the others that will per-haps reveal why this people in this place, this community, are trying to read Scripture and probe its message. In short, the com-mentary, criticism or discussion, constantly refers back to the act which brought it into being. The question of method gives way to the question "Why?"; the method's only purpose was to provoke that question and, in a sense, to ensure its validity. History, ethics, symbols, each plays its part in turn, and the facts of Scripture and the facts of today become mixed. All this constantly brings up again the meaning of such an inquiry, even in the way it is conducted. Whether the means is history, symbols or ethics it is the same people looking for its faith and fidelity to that faith, which can be traced, certainly, but goes beyond description; for norms of conduct, certainly, but going beyond the details of casuistry; for meaning in particular symbols of its own, but going beyond those symbols.

The result is that the old naïvety which was destroyed gives way to another naïvety or, more accurately, reveals the shape and possibility of it. This is no longer the opposition between a "spiritual" and a critical approach, or between a positive and a religious one. In fact, perhaps sticking at the letter would today be a refusal of that confrontation, and a lapse into repetition, which would be no less dead for being spiritual. Confrontation with the message, on the other hand, in a strictly critical attitude, may perhaps enable us to see that the word is not a dead letter but spirit and life.

The table is set. The hungry are numerous. Too many foods are offered elsewhere. It is the task of the Christian communities to see if they can reveal the uniqueness of what they have received, no longer regretting the bygone days when the Church alone controlled the distribution of the Bible, or setting one approach against another, but able to turn the words of the past into Life.

Translated by Francis McDonagh

Biographical Notes

Jacques Audinet was born in 1928. He studied at the Institut Catholique (Paris), at the Sorbonne and at Chicago University. Licentiate in sociology, doctor of theology, he is director of the Institut Supérieur de pastorale catéchétique and professor of theology at the Institut Catholique (Paris). Among his published works are: *Vers une catéchèse des adolescents* (Paris, 1964) and (with Odile Dubuisson) *Conduis-moi sur le chemin de ta maison* (Paris, 1962).

Bruno Dreher was born 24 December 1911 in Leinzell (Germany) and ordained in 1936. Doctor of theology, he is professor of kerygmatics and of pedagogy of religion at the University of Vienna. Among his published works are: *Predigtwerk über die neue Perikopenordnung* (20 vols., of which 8 have been published up to 1971) and *Theologische Erwachsenenbildung* (1969).

Gotthold Hasenhüttl was born 2 December 1933 in Graz (Austria) and was ordained in 1959. He studied at the University of Graz, at the Gregorian (Rome) and at Basle, Zurich, Marburg and Tübingen. Licentiate in philosophy, doctor of theology, he is assistant at the Institute of Ecumenical Research in Tübingen. Among his published works are: *Geschichte und existenziales Denken* (1965); *Charisma: Ordnungsprinzip der Kirche* (1969) and *Gefährdet die moderne Exetese den Glauben?* (1970).

Bas van Iersel, s.m.m., was born 27 September 1924 in Heerlen (Netherlands) and ordained in 1950. He studied at the Universities of Nijmegen and Louvain. Doctor of theology, he is reader of the New Testament at the University of Nijmegen. Among his published works is *"Der Sohn" in den synoptischen Jesusworten* (Leyden, 1961).

Meinrad Limbeck was born in 1934. He studied philosophy and theology at Tübingen and Bonn. Doctor of theology, he is assistant at the Faculty of Catholic Theology at the University of Tübingen. Among his published works are: *Die Ordnung des Heils* (Düsseldorf, 1971) and *Kommentar zum Markus-Evangelium* (Stuttgart, 1968[4]).

OSWALD LORETZ was born 14 January 1928 in Horbranz (Germany) and is a priest. He studied at the Gregorian and the Pontifical Biblical Institute in Rome and at Chicago University. Doctor of theology, licentiate in Sacred Scripture, he is professor at the Westfälische Wilhelms University. Among his published works are: *Gotteswort und menschliche Erfahrung* (Freiburg, 1963) and *Qohelet und der Alte Orient* (Freiburg, 1964).

RODERICK MACKENZIE, S.J., is a Canadian. Master of arts and doctor of Sacred Scripture, he is professor of Old Testament exegesis at the Pontifical Biblical Institute (Rome) and editor of *Biblica*. Among his published works are: *Faith and History in the Old Testament* (1963), *The Psalms: A Selection* (1967) and *The Book of Job* in *The Jerome Biblical Commentary* (1968).

CARL PETER was born 4 April 1932 in Omaha and was ordained in 1951. He studied in Rome at the Gregorian and the St Thomas Aquinas University. Doctor of Philosophy and of theology, he is associate professor of systematic theology at the Catholic University of America (Washington). Among his published works is *Participated Eternity in the Vision of God* (Rome, 1964).

LUIS ALONSO SCHÖKEL, S.J., was born 15 February 1920 in Madrid and ordained in 1949. He studied at the Faculty of Philosophy in Burgos, at Comillas University (Santander) and at the Pontifical Biblical Institute (Rome). Licentiate in philosophy and in theology, doctor of Sacred Scripture, he is professor of introduction to the Old Testament and of biblical theology at the Pontifical Biblical Institute (Rome). Among his published works are: *La palabra inspirada* (1966) and *Comentarios a la constitucion Dei Verbum*.

PIET SCHOONENBERG, S.J., was born 1 October 1911 in Amsterdam and ordained in 1939. He studied at the Faculty of Theology in Maestricht and at the Pontifical Biblical Institute (Rome). Doctor of theology, he is professor of dogmatics at the University of Nijmegen. Among his published works are: *Het geloof van ons doopsel* (4 vols. have appeared) and *Gods Wordende Wereld* (Tielt, 1962).

GERHARD VOSS, O.S.B., was born 25 July 1935 in Recklinghausen (Germany) and ordained in 1961. He studied at the Universities of Münster, Innsbruck and Würzburg. Doctor of theology, he is manager of the Ecumenical Institute of the Abbey of Niederaltaich (Germany) and a contributor to the ecumenical review *Una Sancta*. Among his published works are: *Die Christologie der lukanischen Scriften in Grundzügen* (Paris/Bruges, 1965) and "Die ökumenische Bedeutung der biblischen Hermeneutik" in *Una Sancta* (Nos. 1/2, 1968).

ROBERT WARE, C.S.CR., was born 24 December 1938 in Chicago and ordained in 1964. He studied at the Universities of Notre Dame, Nijmegen and Heidelberg and at the Gregorian (Rome). He has taught at St Mary's College, Omaha and has given courses in Germany and Switzerland. At present he is preparing a thesis for the doctorate of theology on the interpretation of the Resurrection. He has contributed to *Tijdschrift voor Theologie, Theological Studies, The Catholic World* and *The Priest*.

JOSEPH ZALOTAY was born 7 September 1926 in Budapest and was ordained in 1951. He studied theology at Vác (Hungary), at the University of Vienna and at the Pontifical Biblical Institute (Rome). Doctor of theology, licentiate in Sacred Scripture, he is associate professor of the New Testament at the Catholic University of America (Washington).

International Publishers of CONCILIUM

ENGLISH EDITION
Herder and Herder Inc.
New York, U.S.A.

Burns & Oates Ltd.
P.O. Box 497,
London, S.W.7

DUTCH EDITION
Uitgeverij Paul Brand, N.V.
Hilversum, Netherlands

FRENCH EDITION
Maison Mame
Tours/Paris, France

JAPANESE EDITION (PARTIAL)
Nansôsha
Tokyo, Japan

GERMAN EDITION
Verlagsanstalt Benziger & Co., A.G.
Einsiedeln, Switzerland

Matthias Grunewald-Verlag
Mainz, W. Germany

SPANISH EDITION
Ediciones Cristianidad
Salamanca, Spain

PORTUGUESE EDITION
Livraria Morais Editoria, Ltda.
Lisbon, Portugal

ITALIAN EDITION
Editrice Queriniana
Brescia, Italy

POLISH EDITION (PARTIAL)
Pallottinum
Poznań, Poland